Celtic Designs and Motifs

Courtney Davis

Dover Publications, Inc., *New York*

Celtic Designs and Motifs is a new work, first published by Dover Publications, Inc., in 1991.

DOVER *Pictorial Archive* SERIES

This book belongs to the Dover Pictorial Archive Series. You may use the designs and illustrations for graphics and crafts applications, free and without special permission, provided that you include no more than ten in the same publication or project. For permission for additional use, please email the Permissions Department at rights@doverpublications.com or write to Dover Publications, Inc., 31 East 2nd Street, Mineola, New York 11501.

However, resale, licensing, republication, reproduction or distribution of any illustration by any other graphic service, whether it be in a book or in any other design resource, is strictly prohibited.

Library of Congress Cataloging-in-Publication Data

Davis, Courtney, 1946–
Celtic designs and motifs / Courtney Davis.
p. cm.—(Dover pictorial archive series) (Dover design library)
ISBN 0-486-26718-0 (pbk.)
1. Decoration and ornament, Celtic—Themes, motives. I. Title. II. Series. III. Series: Dover design library.
NK1264.D38 1991
745.4'41'09364—dc20 91-9717
CIP

Printed in Canada
26718016 2025
www.doverpublications.com

Introduction

Arising from a deeply felt consciousness of the interrelatedness of natural and spiritual realms, Celtic art has retained its freshness and vitality over the centuries. In this collection, noted artist and designer Courtney Davis brings you 103 illustrations that convey the essence of Celtic design. His superbly executed renditions are clear, crisp and uncluttered, affording maximum versatility in application. Five types of Celtic decorative art are represented here: involved spiral designs, tilelike step patterns, labyrinthine key motifs, lacy knotwork patterns and zoomorphic (animal and bird) forms. There are numerous variations on these themes, increasing your chances of finding just the right design for your project. And you'll find different shapes for different uses: borders, triangles, circles and corners. The potential applications for this magical art are unlimited. Metalwork, leather, clothing, textiles, graphics and advertising—these represent a fraction of the many things that can be transformed by the designs in this useful collection.

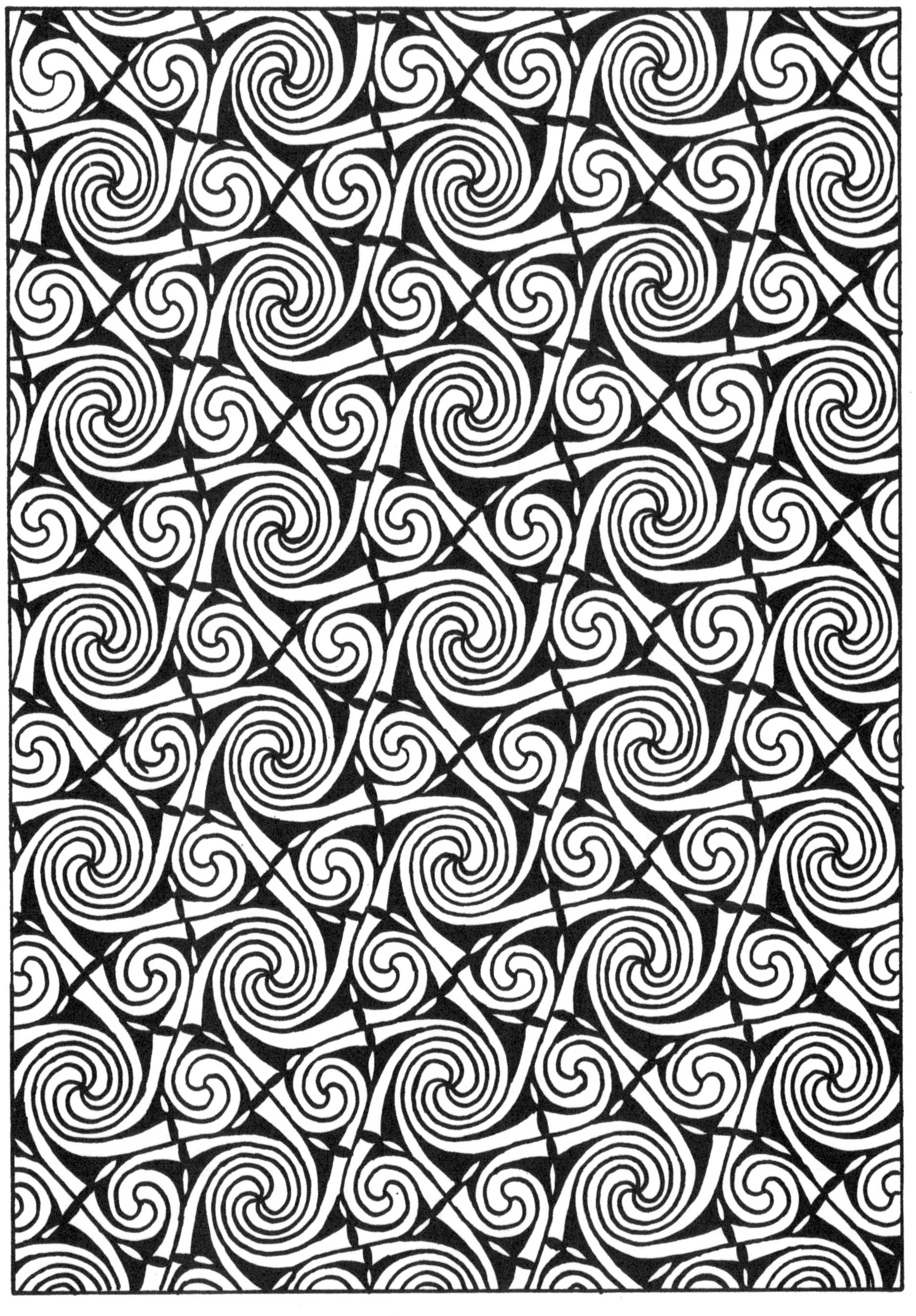

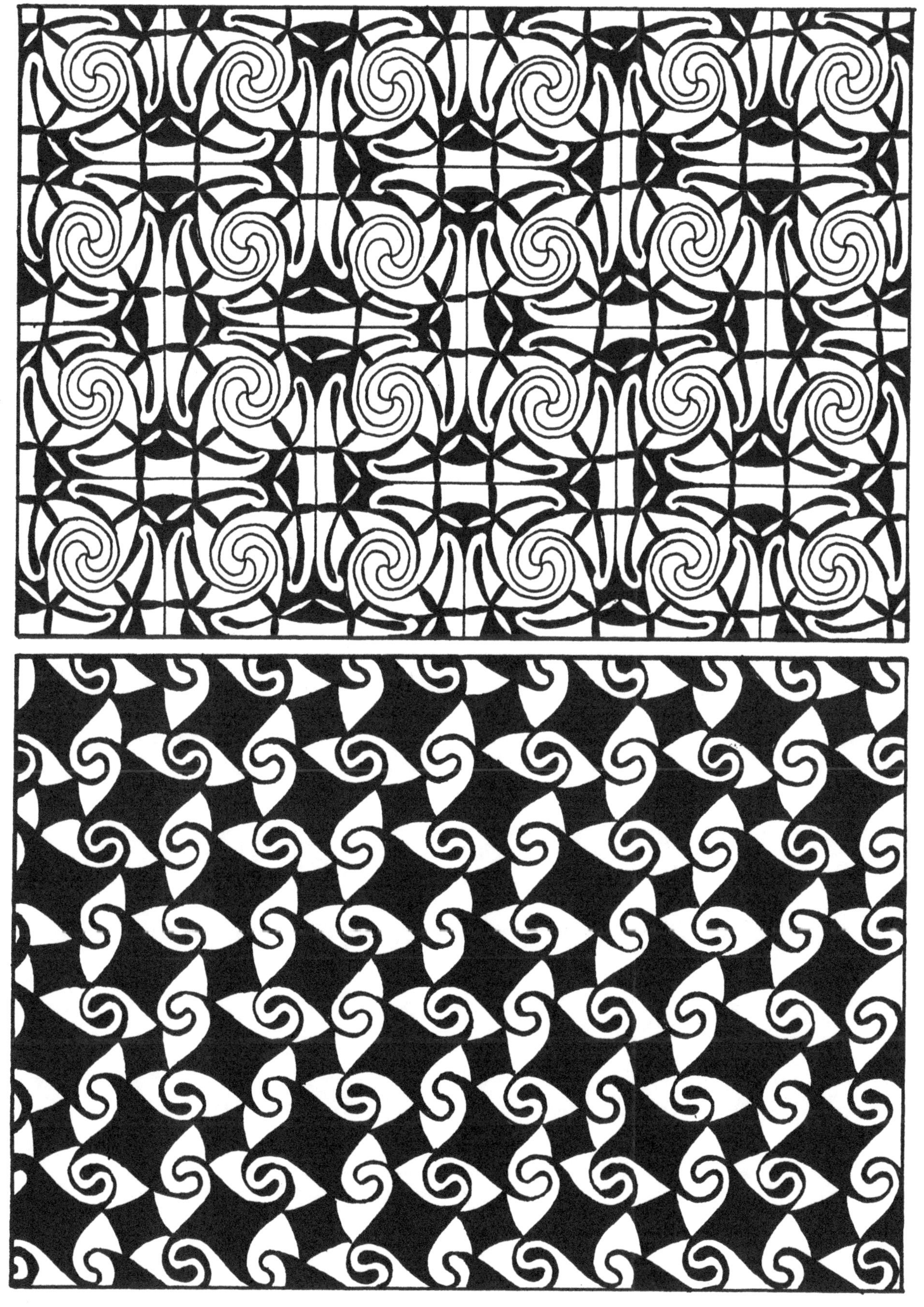

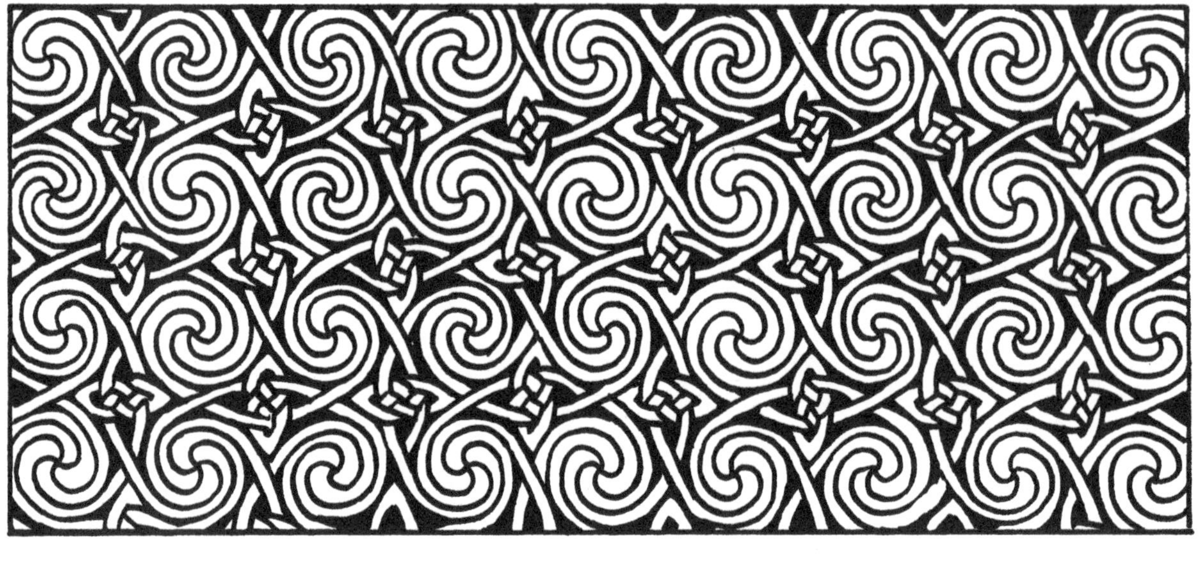

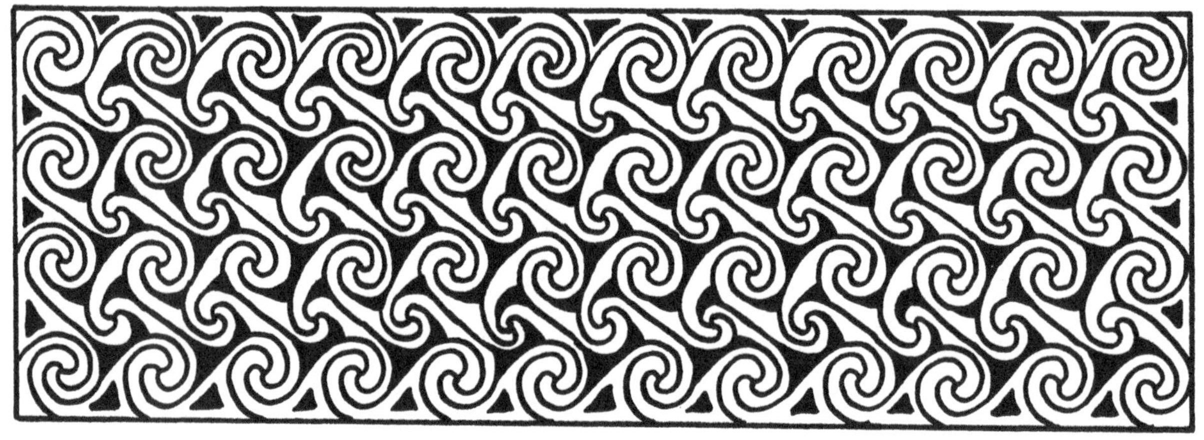

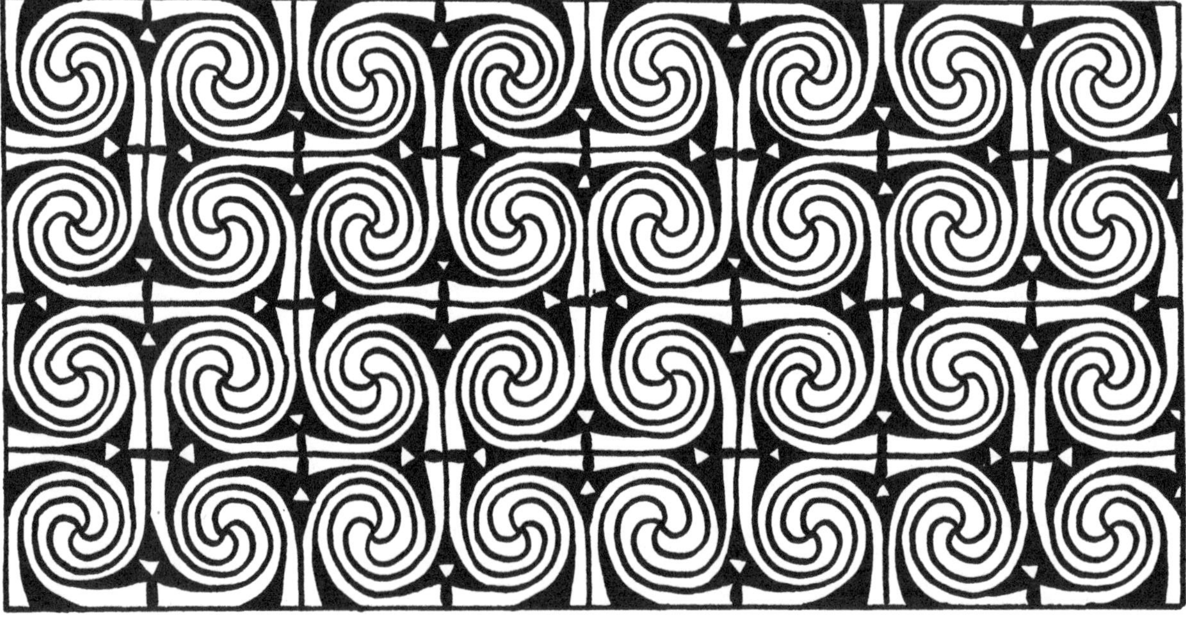

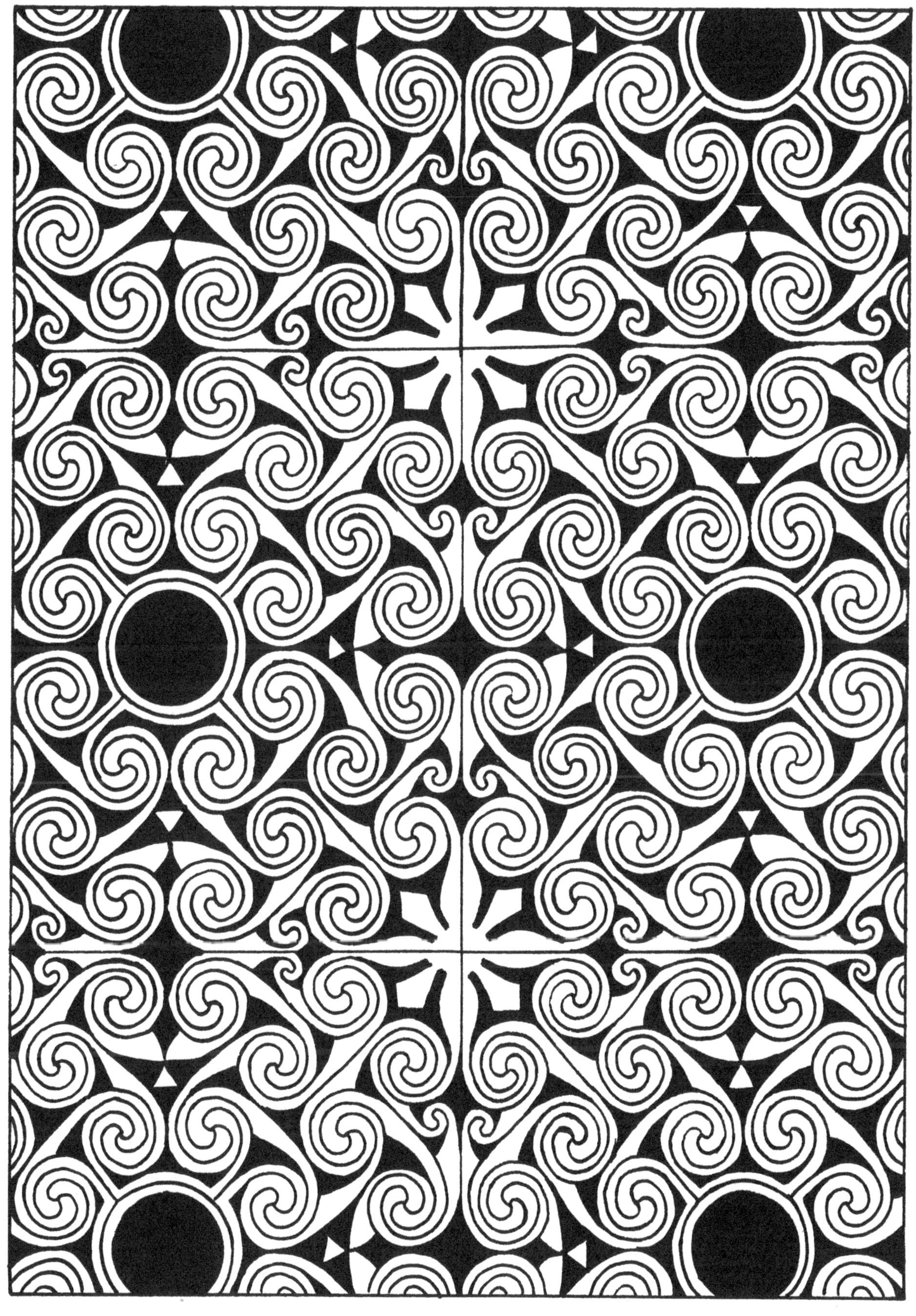

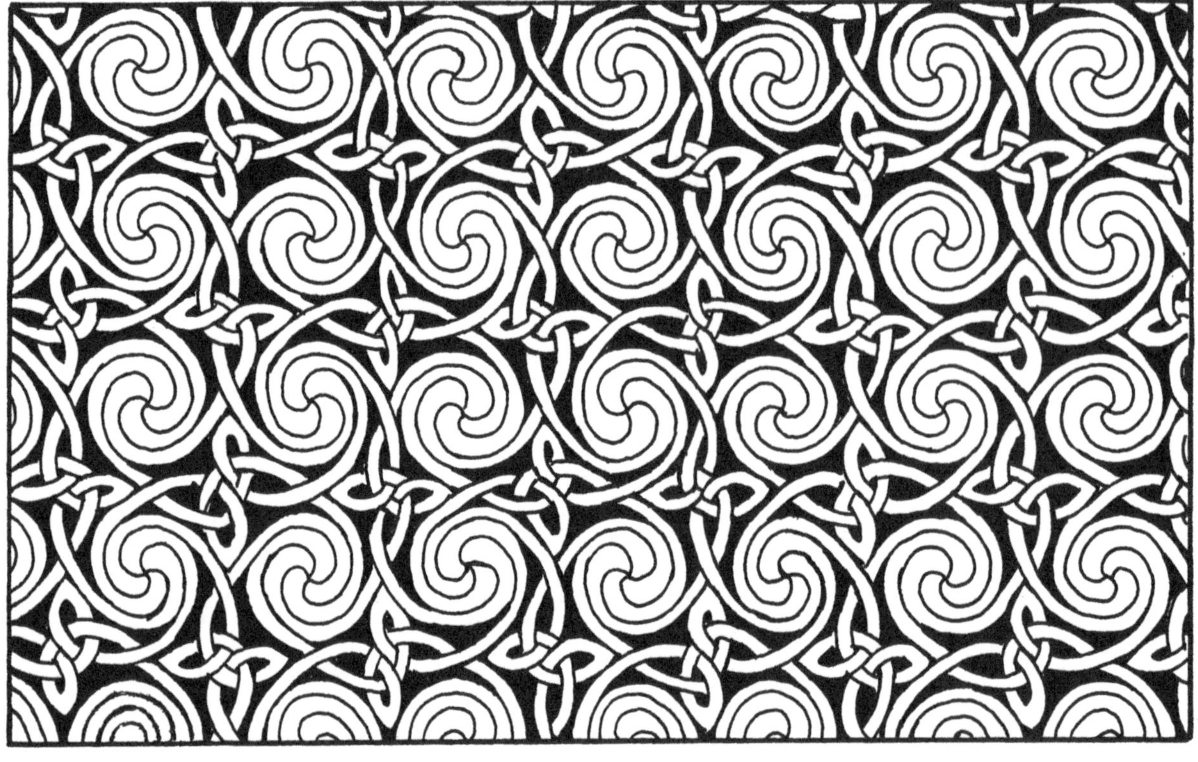

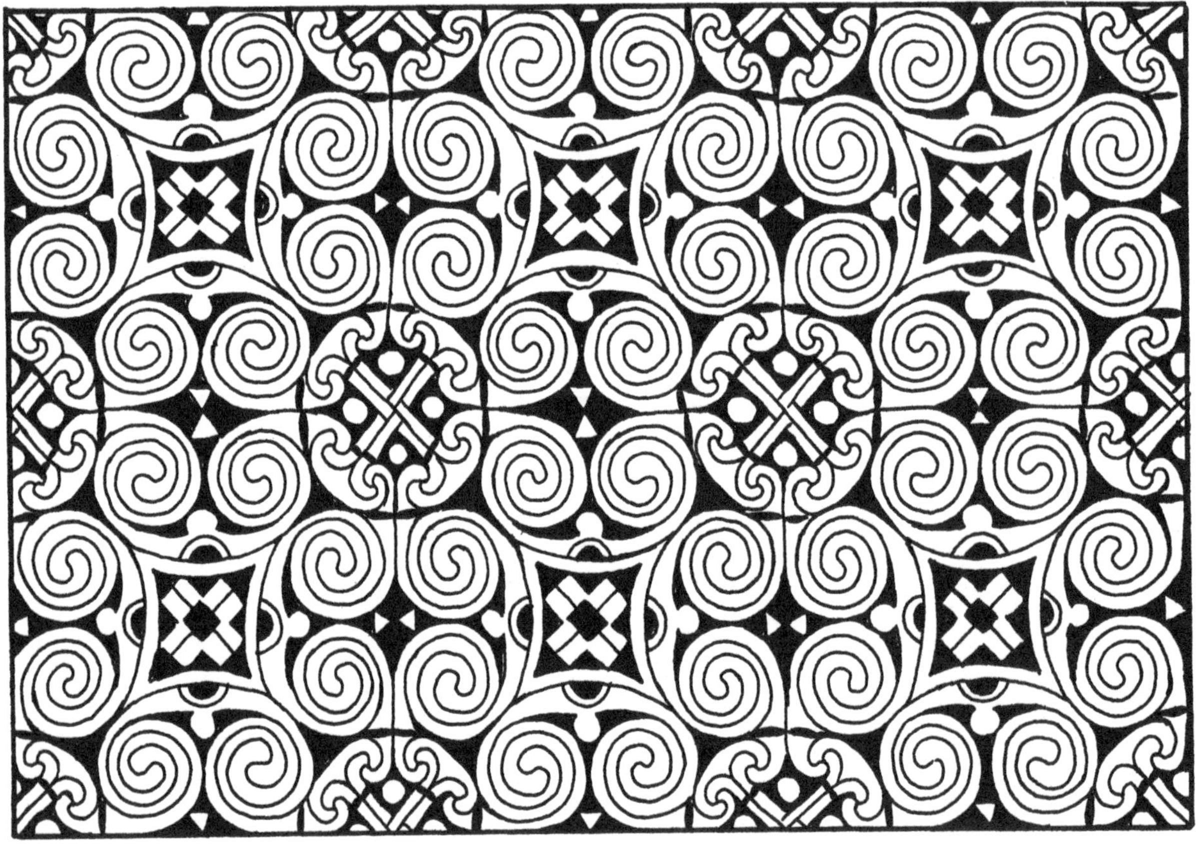

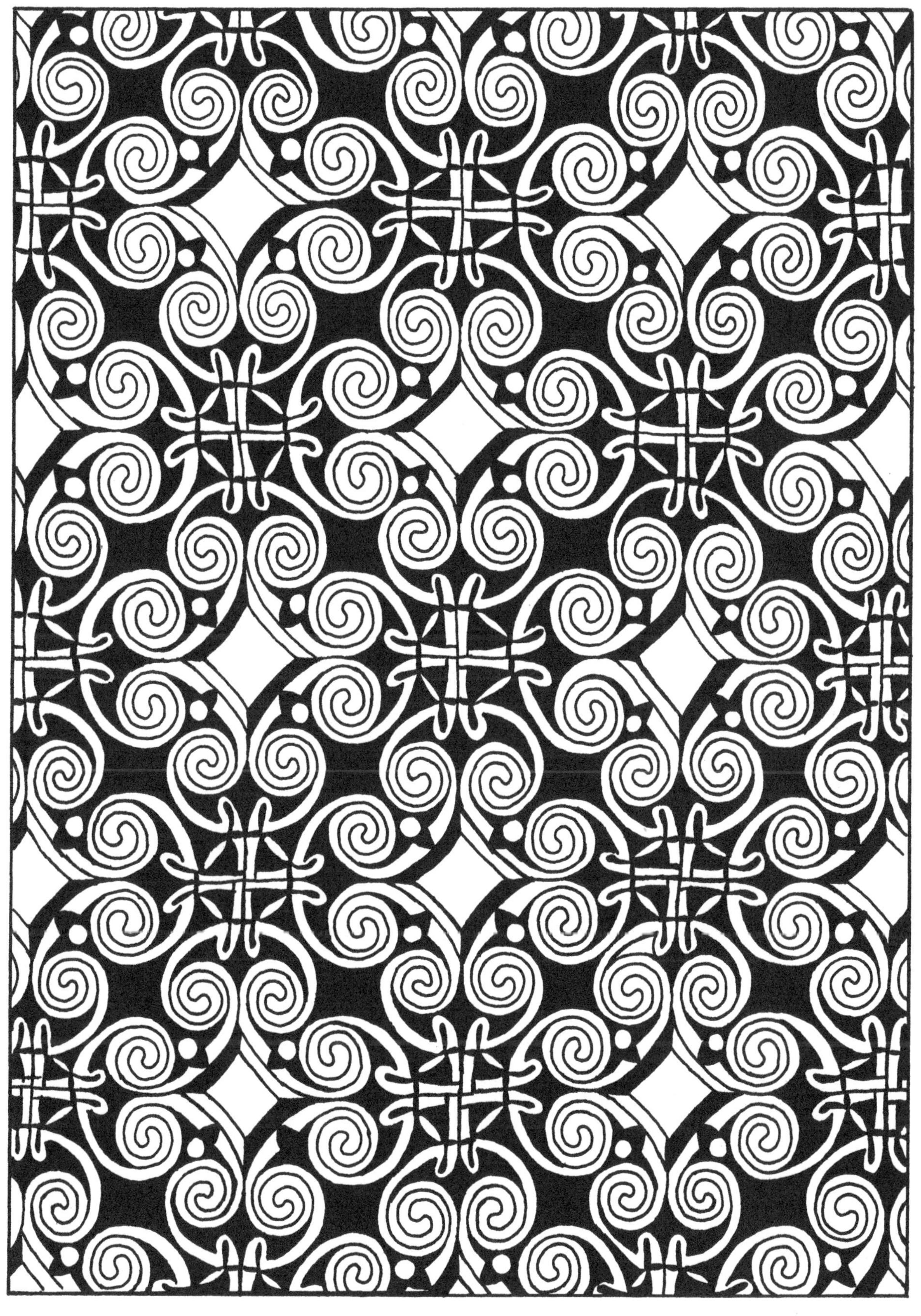

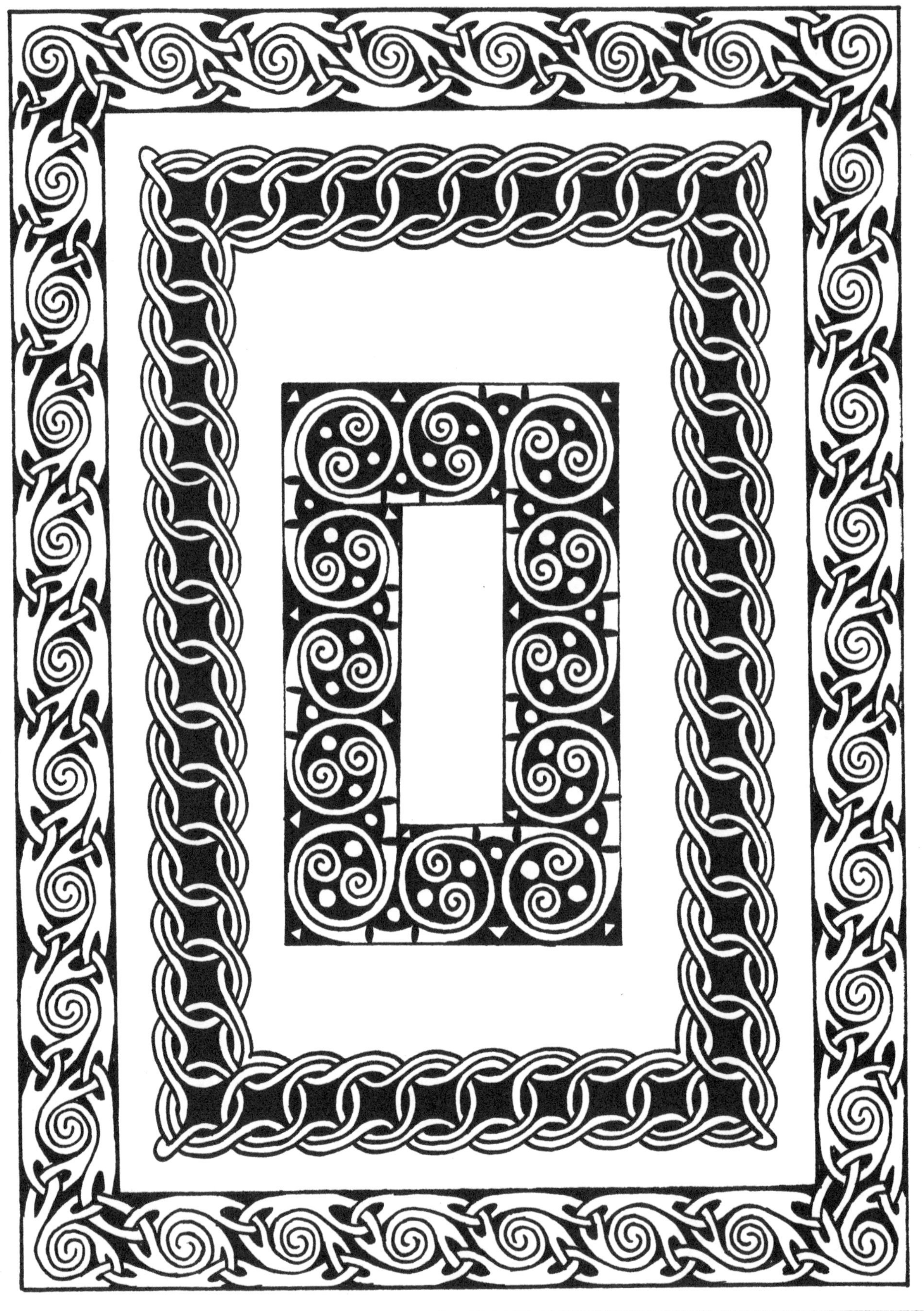

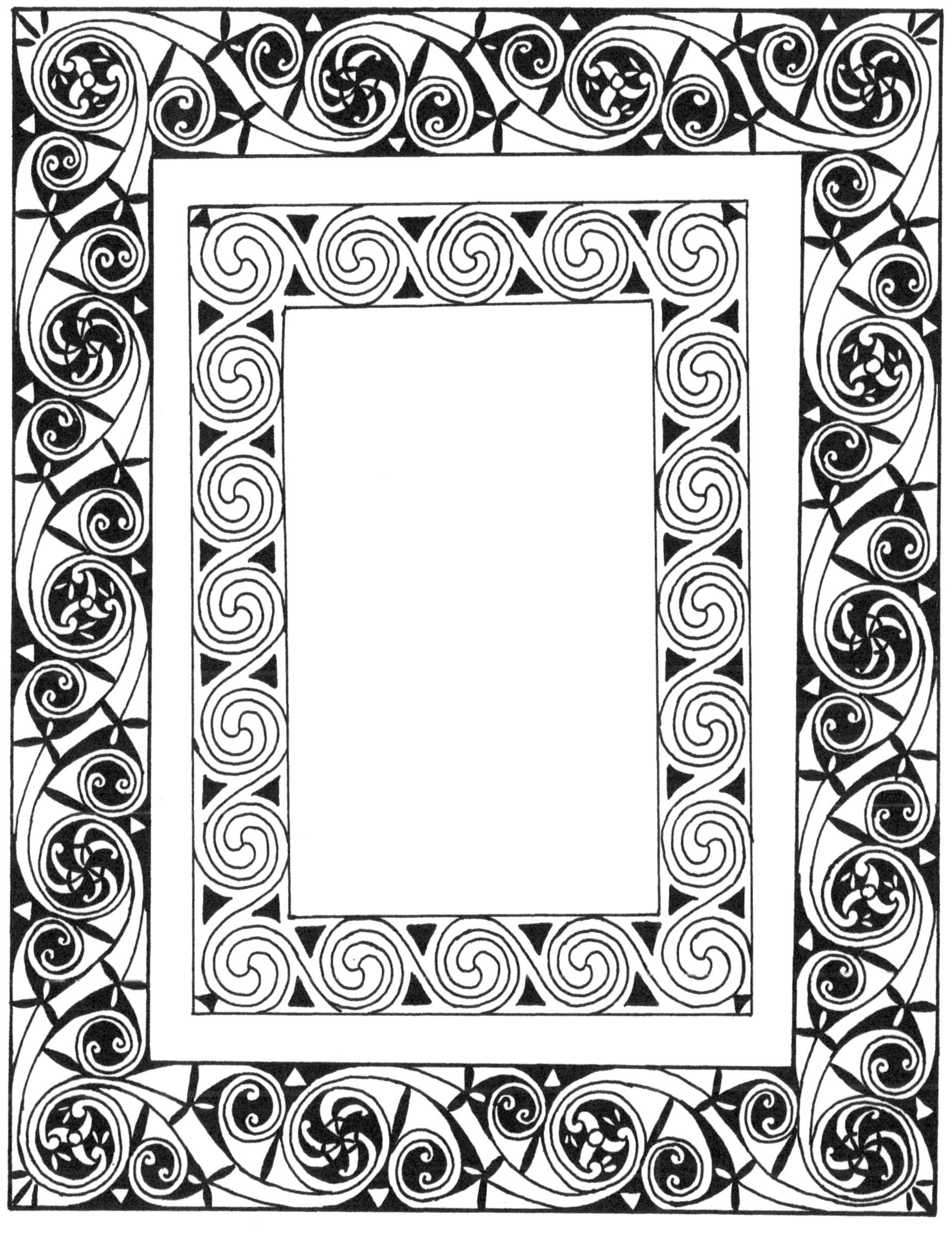

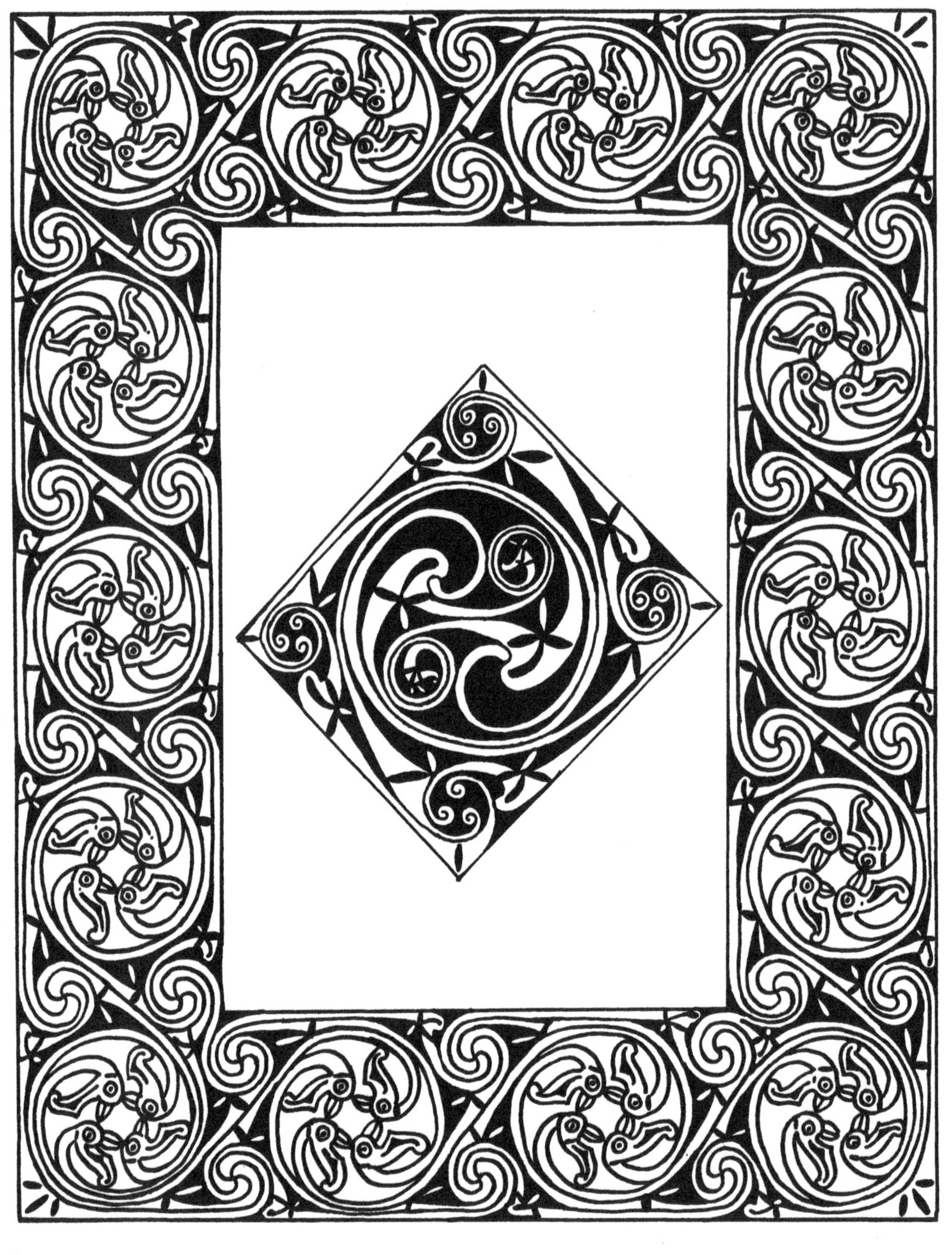

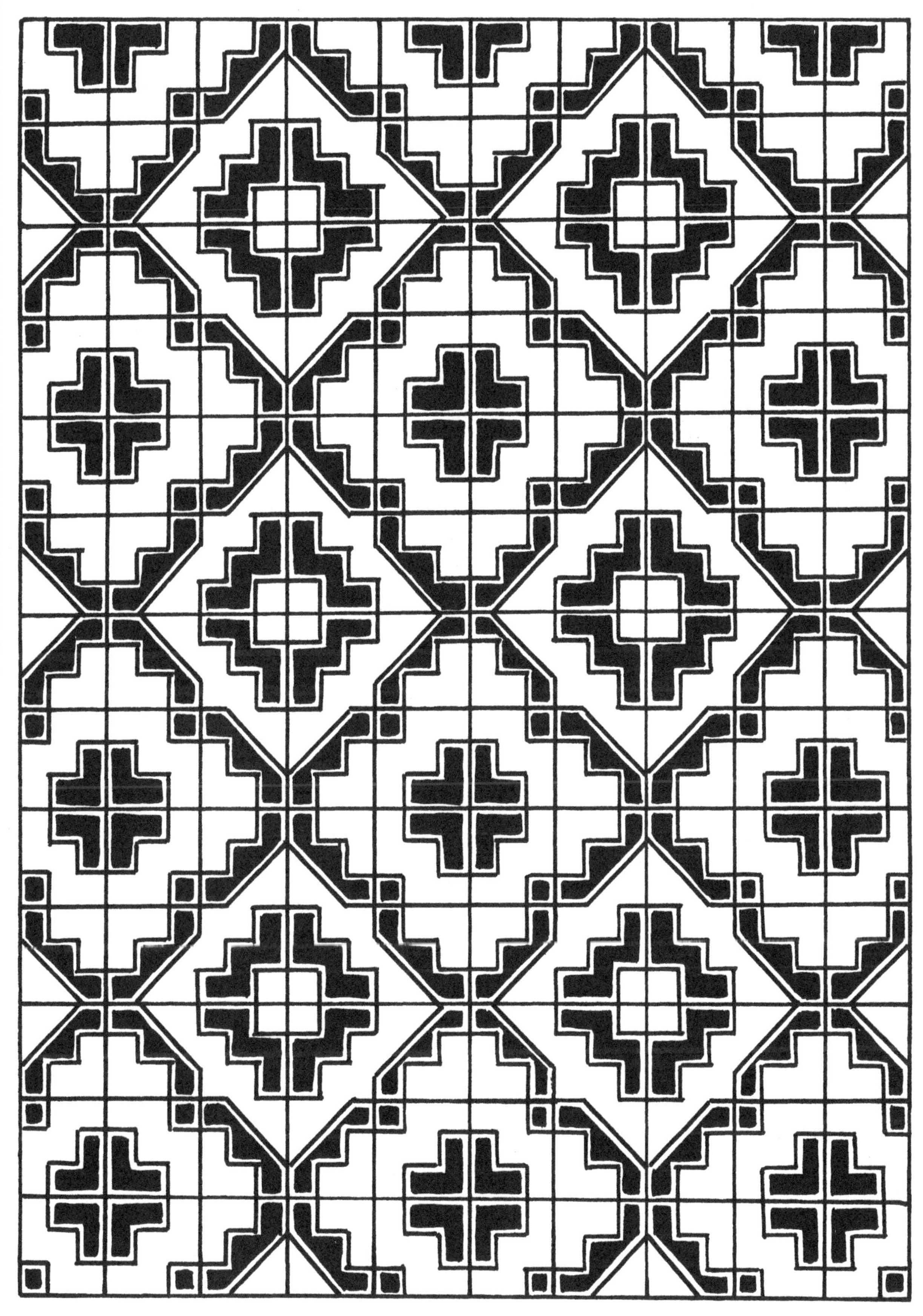

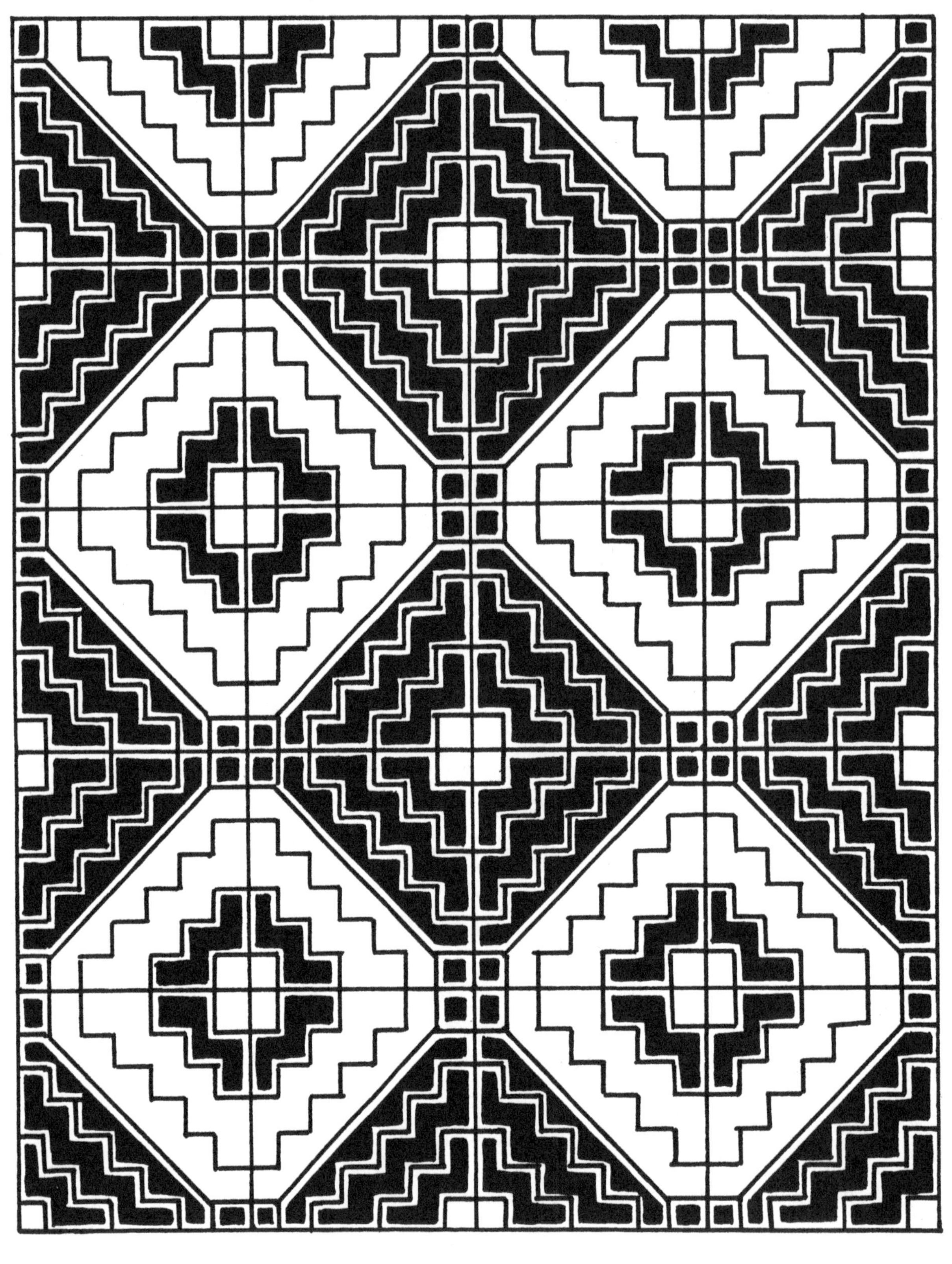

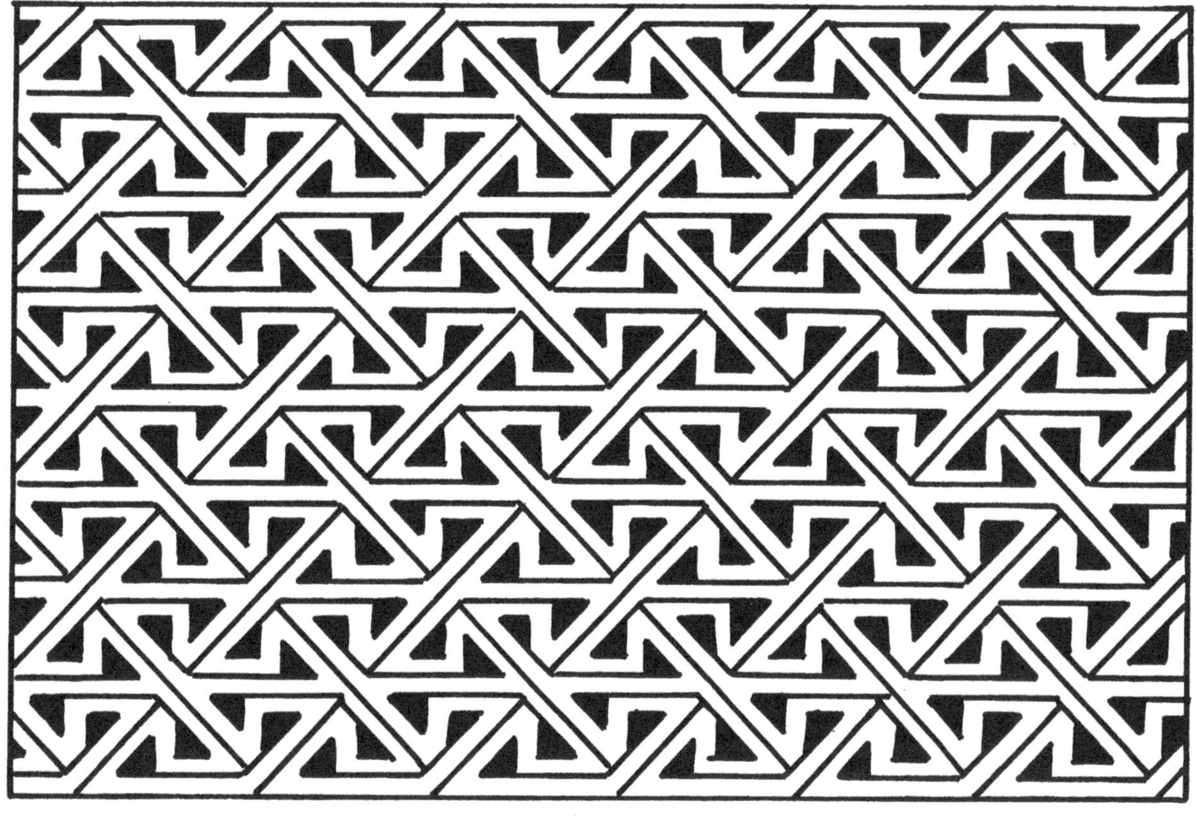

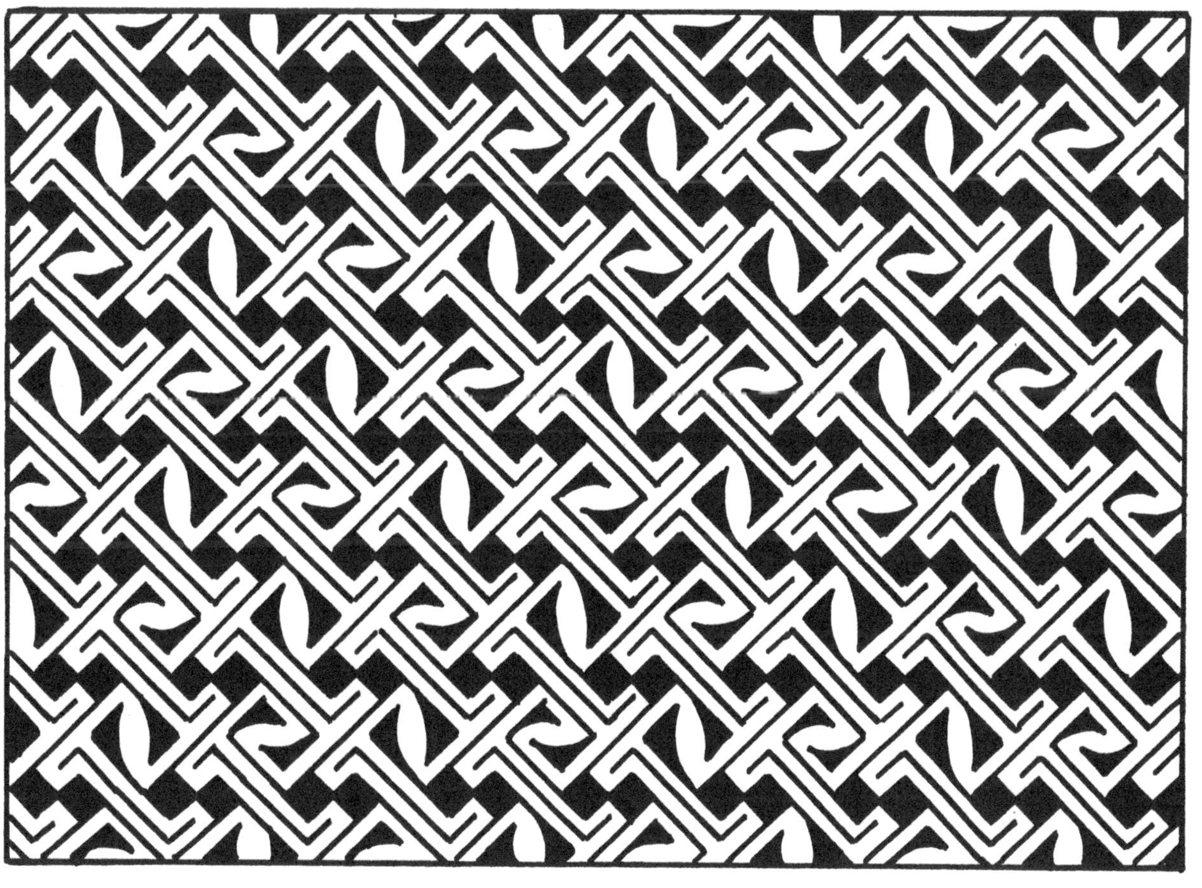

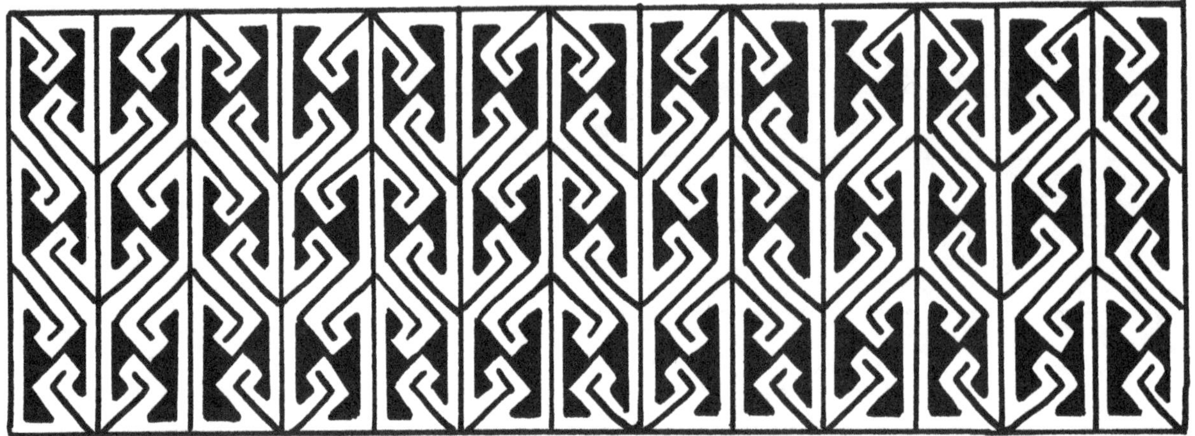

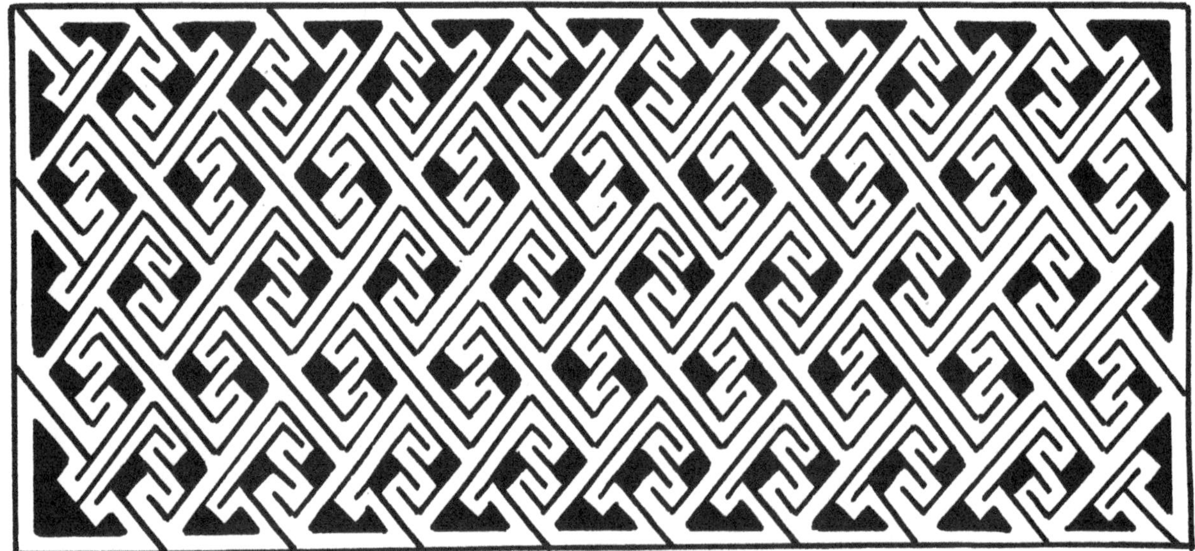

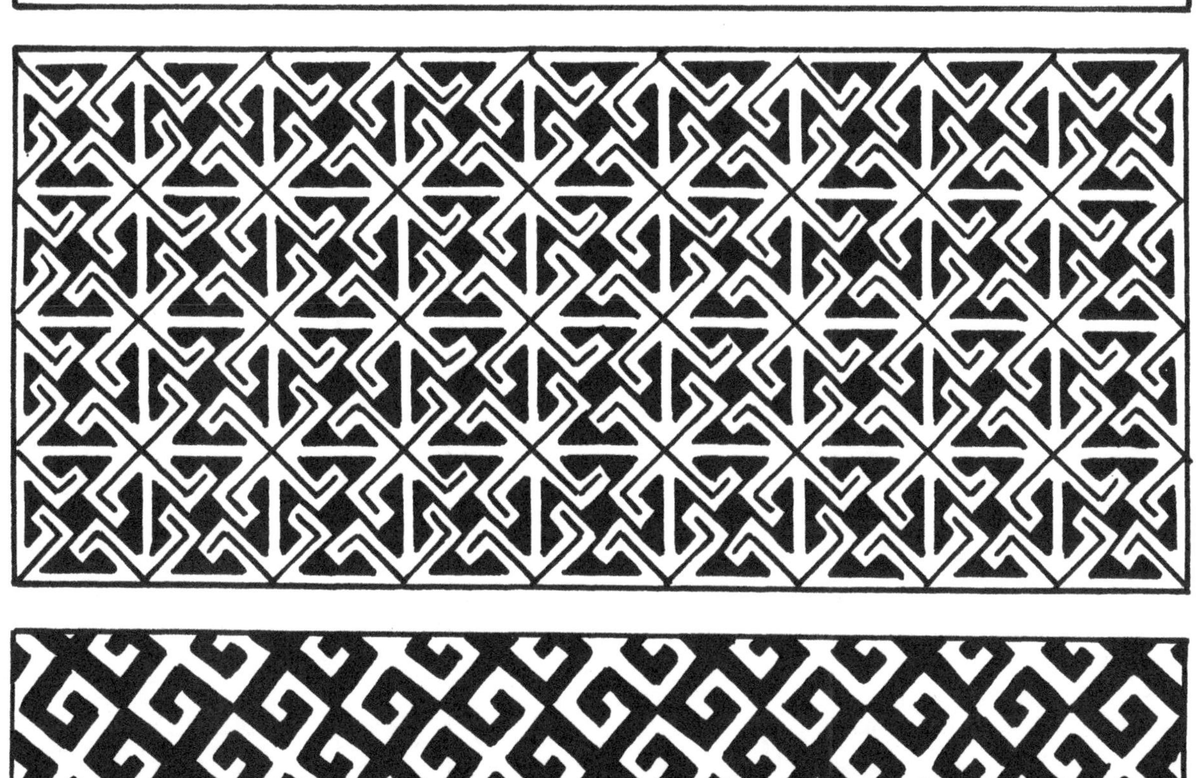

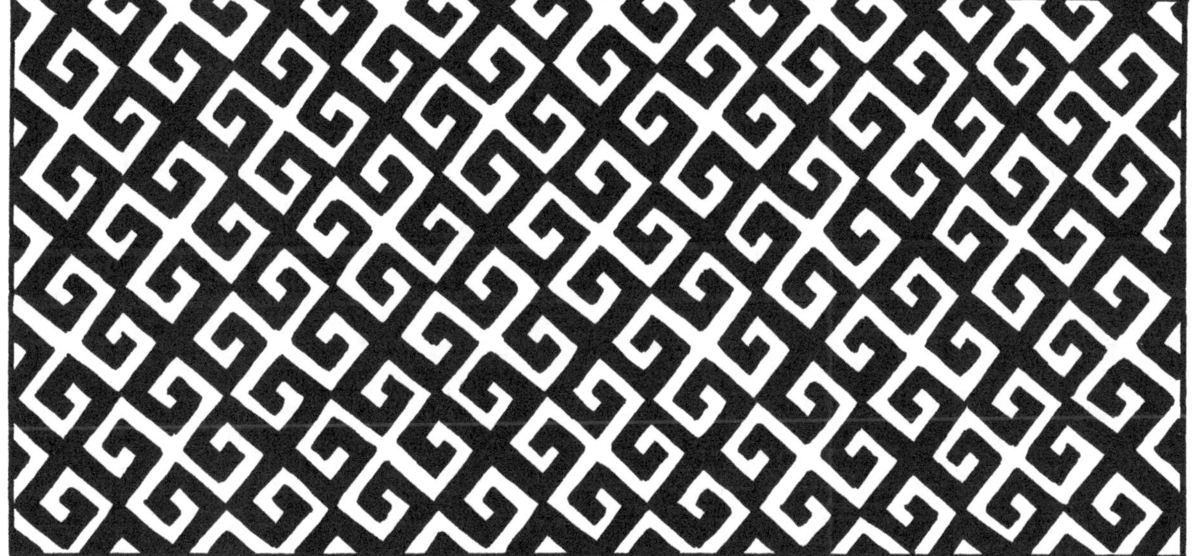

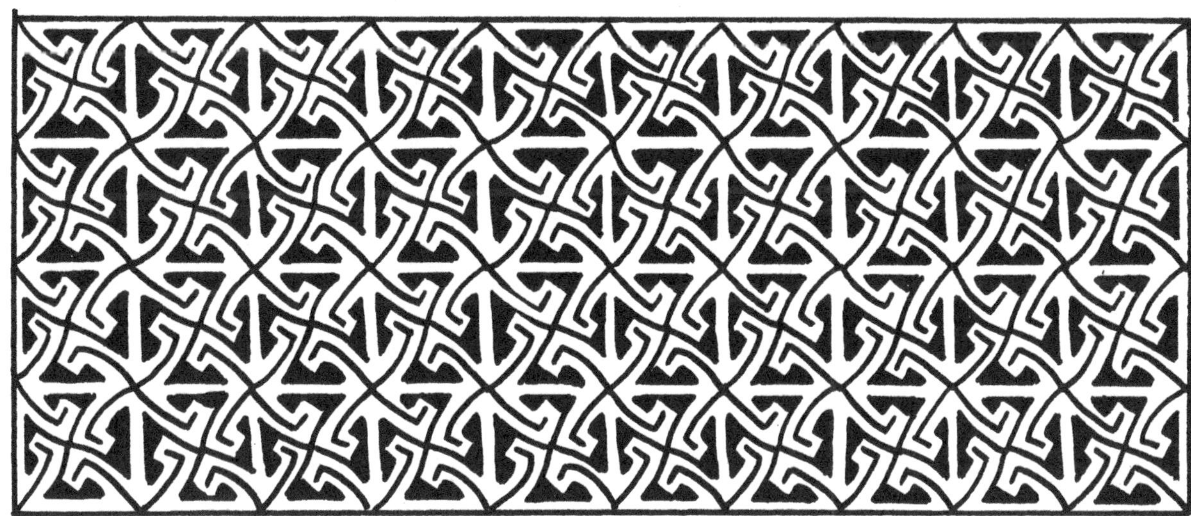

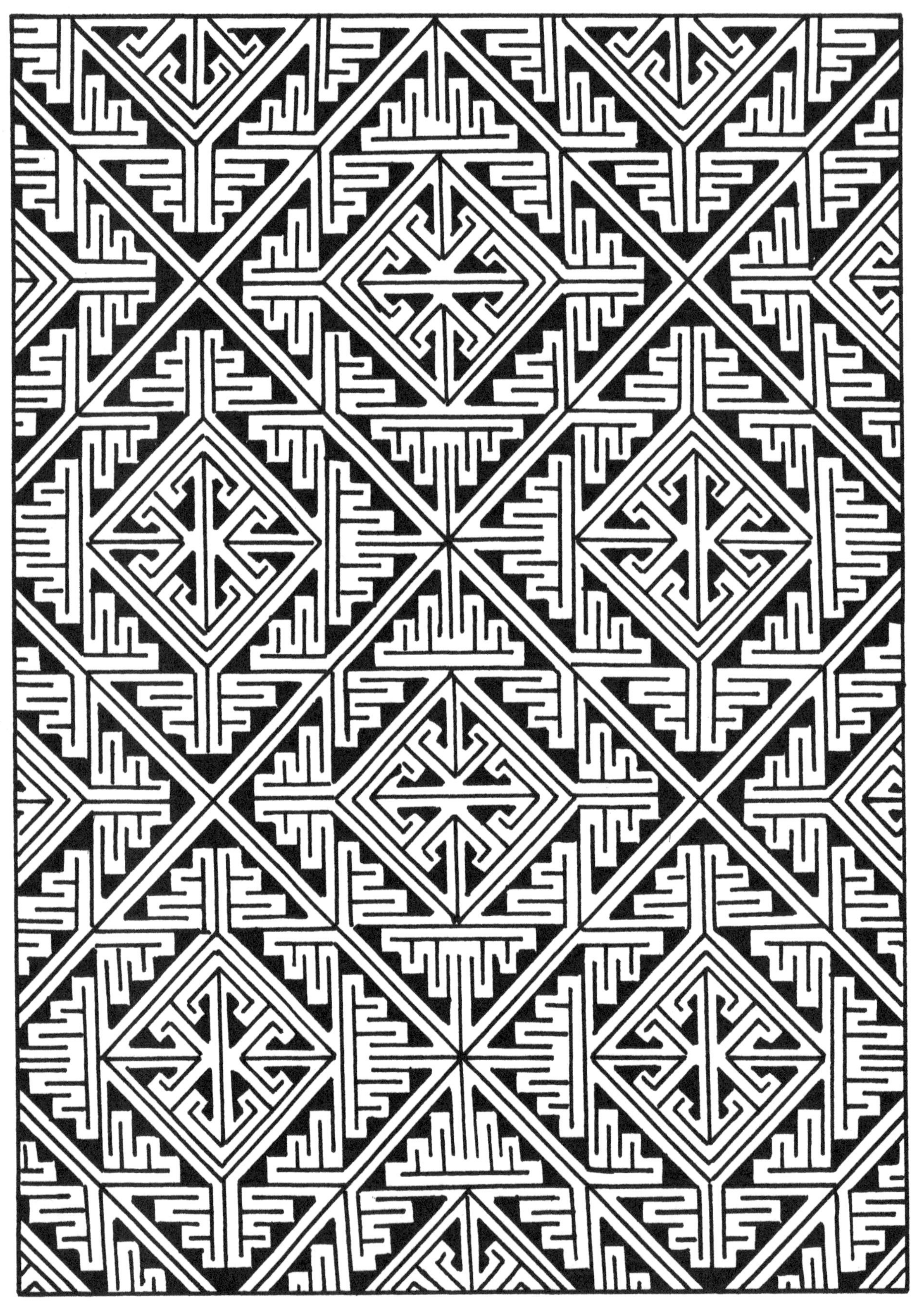

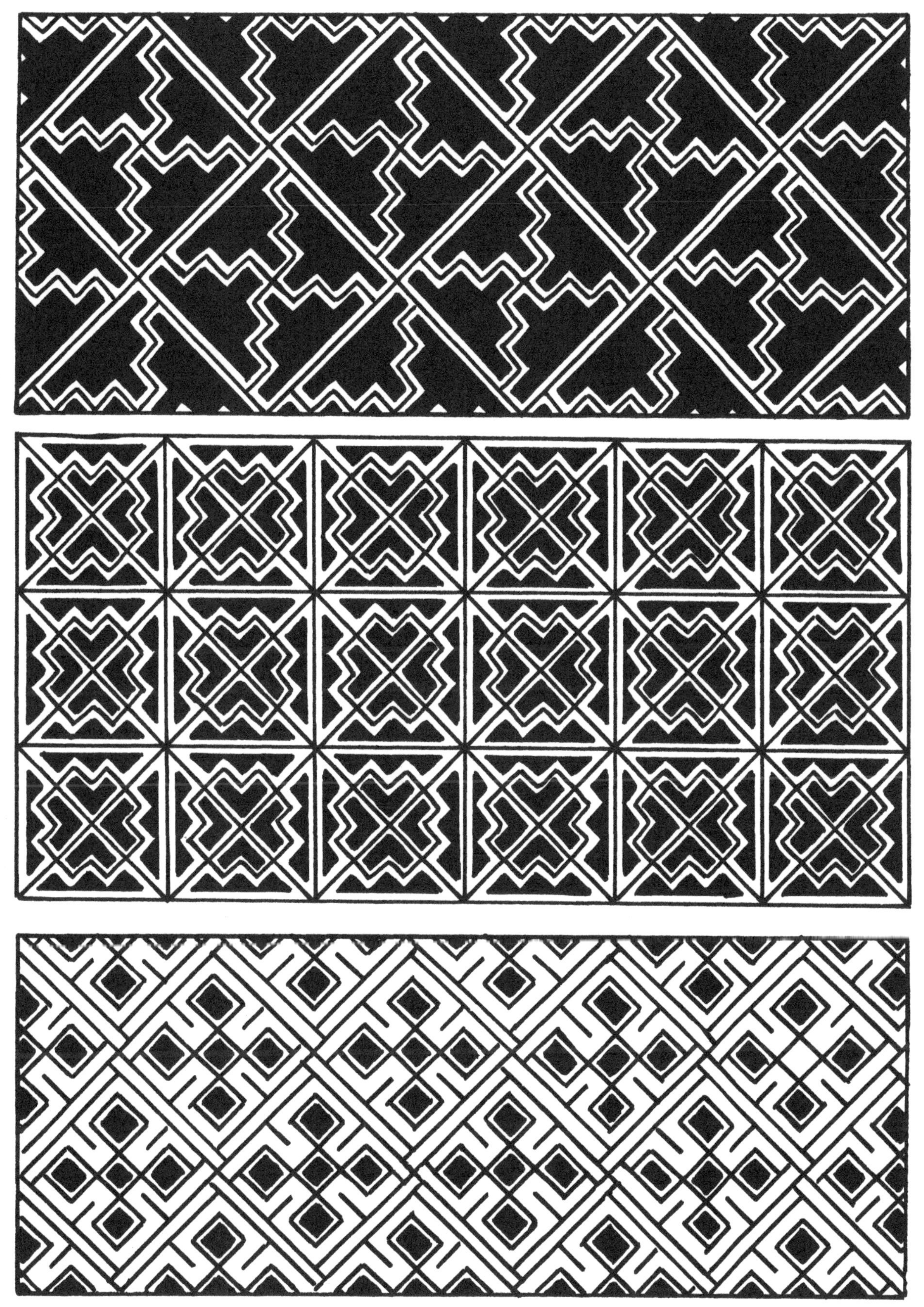

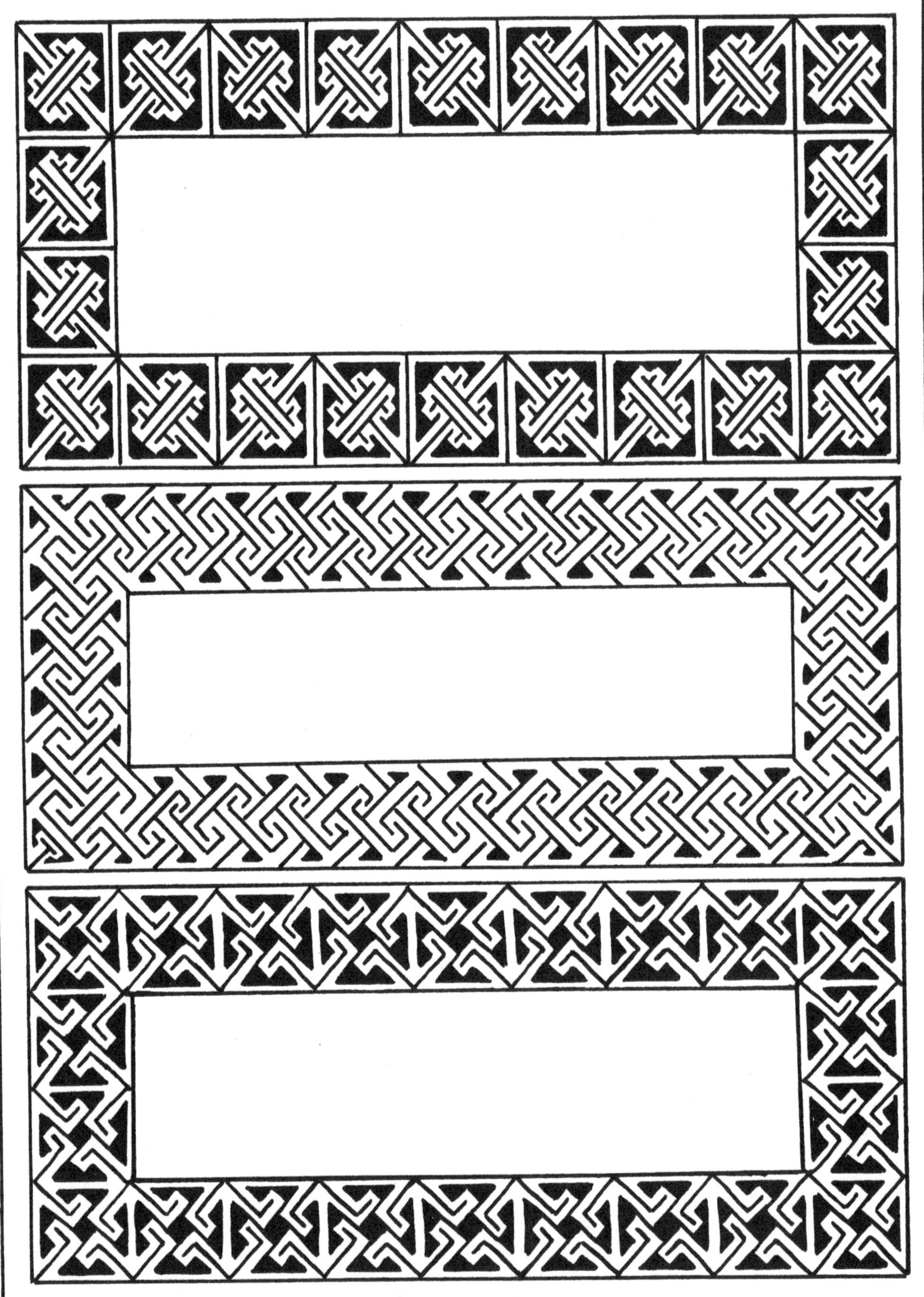

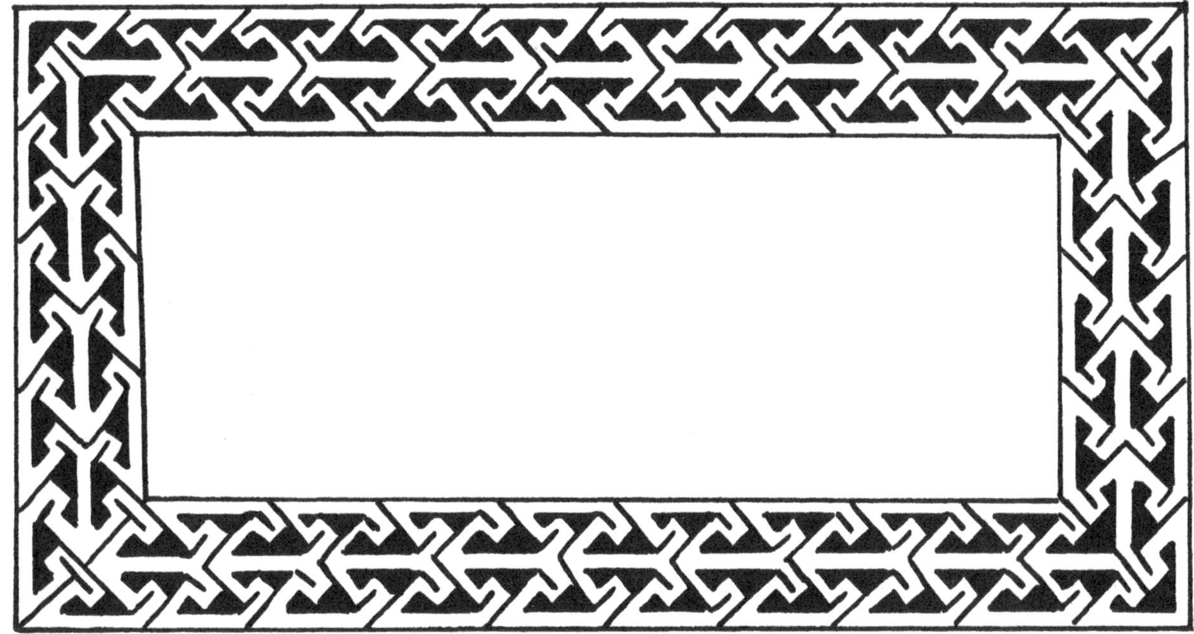

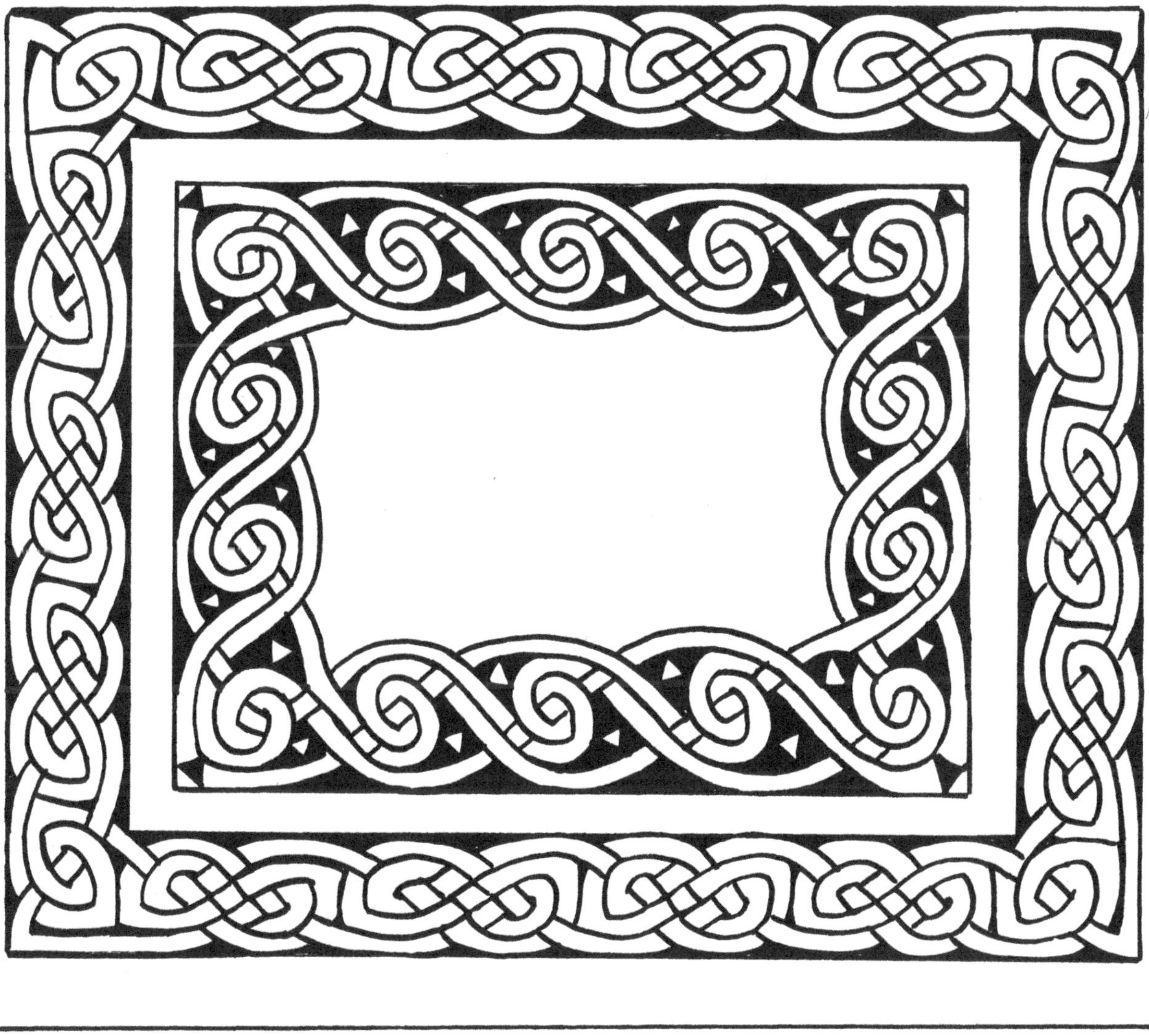

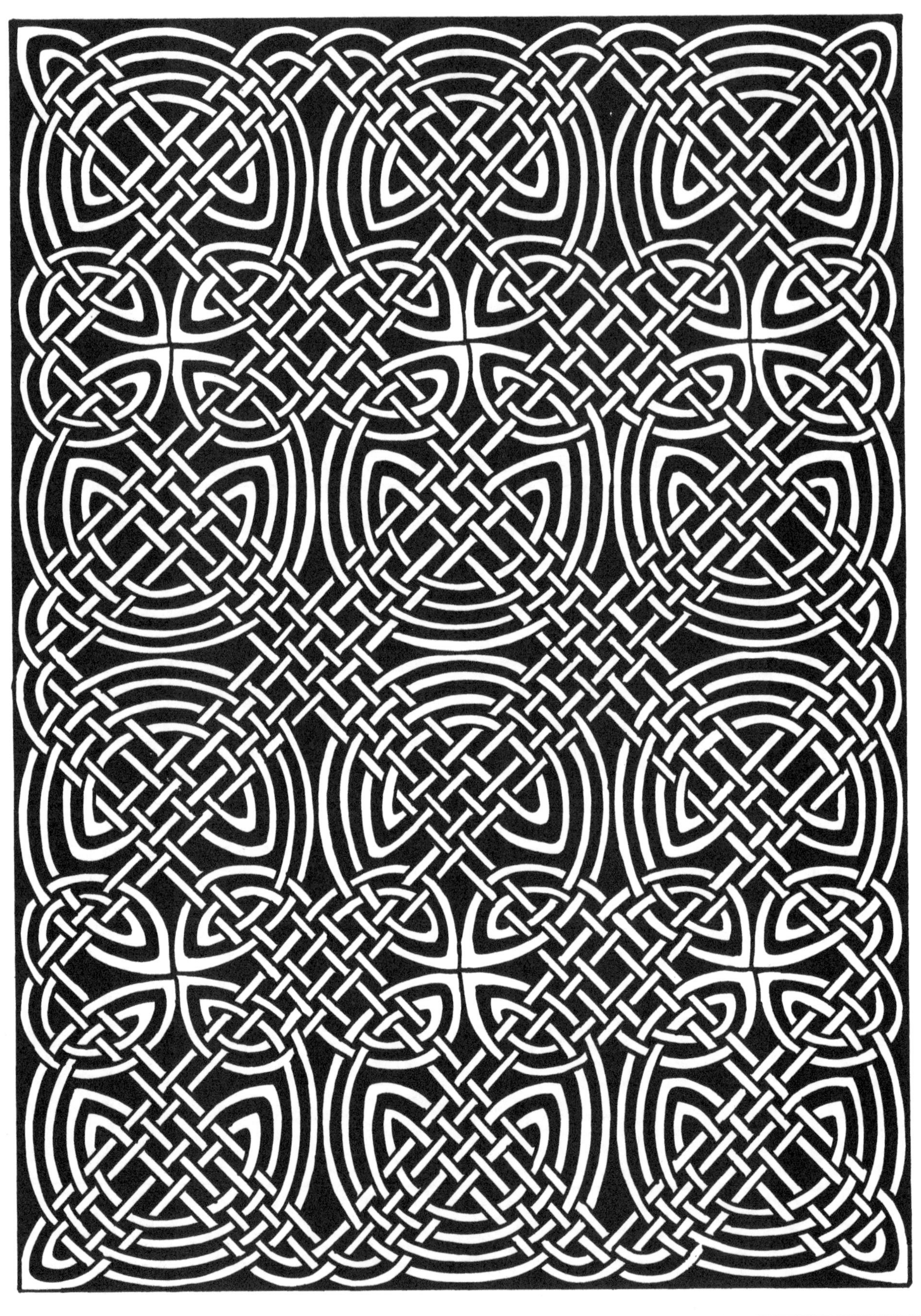

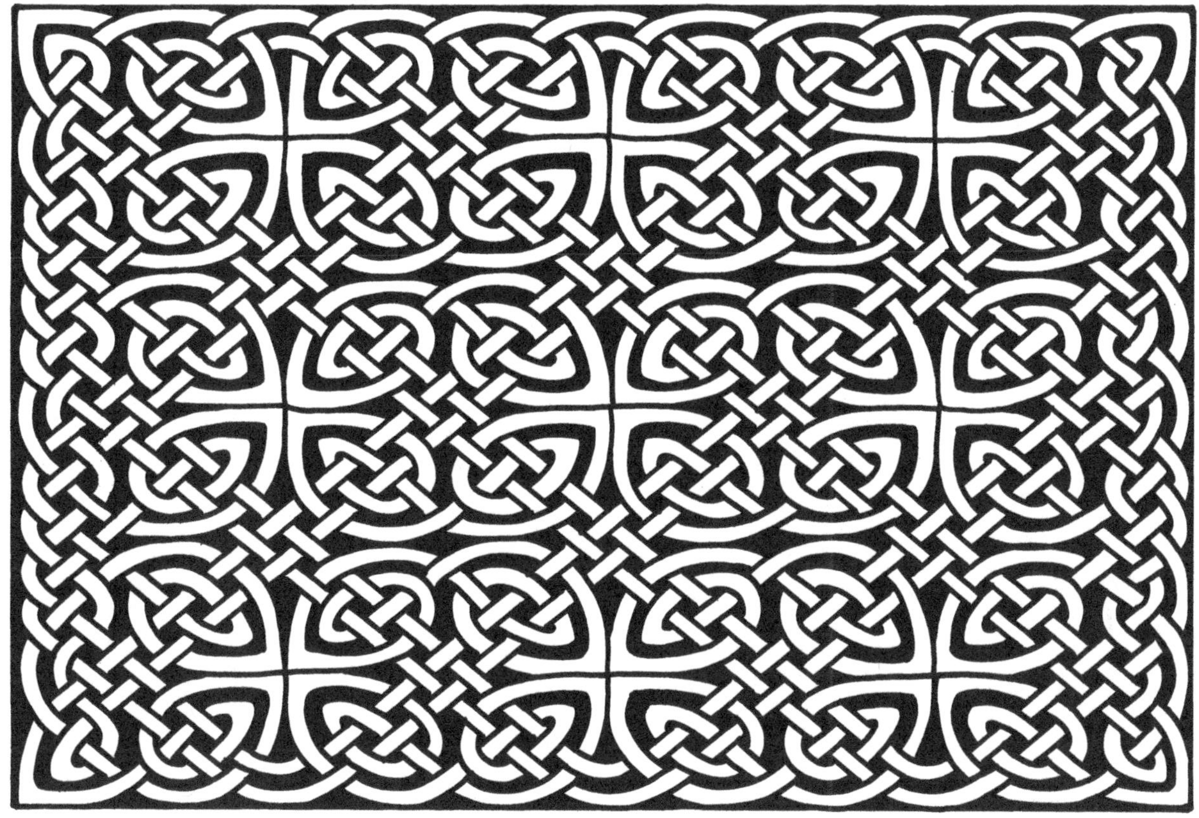

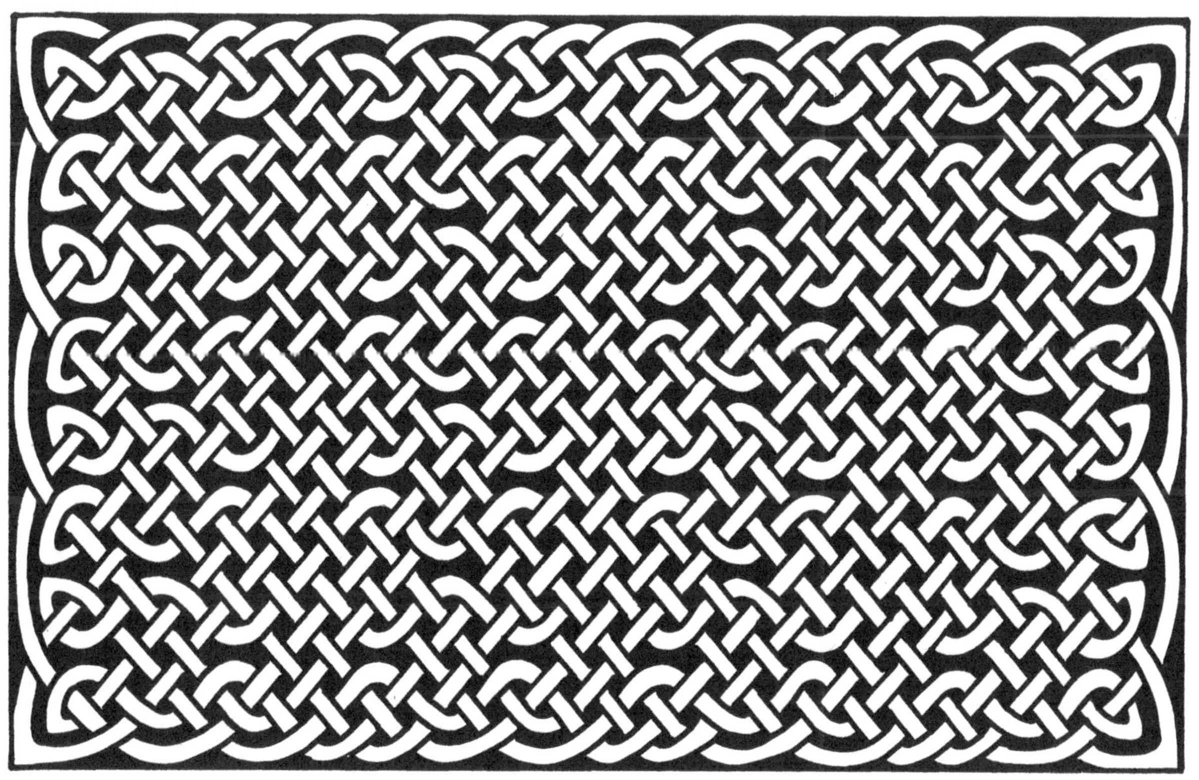

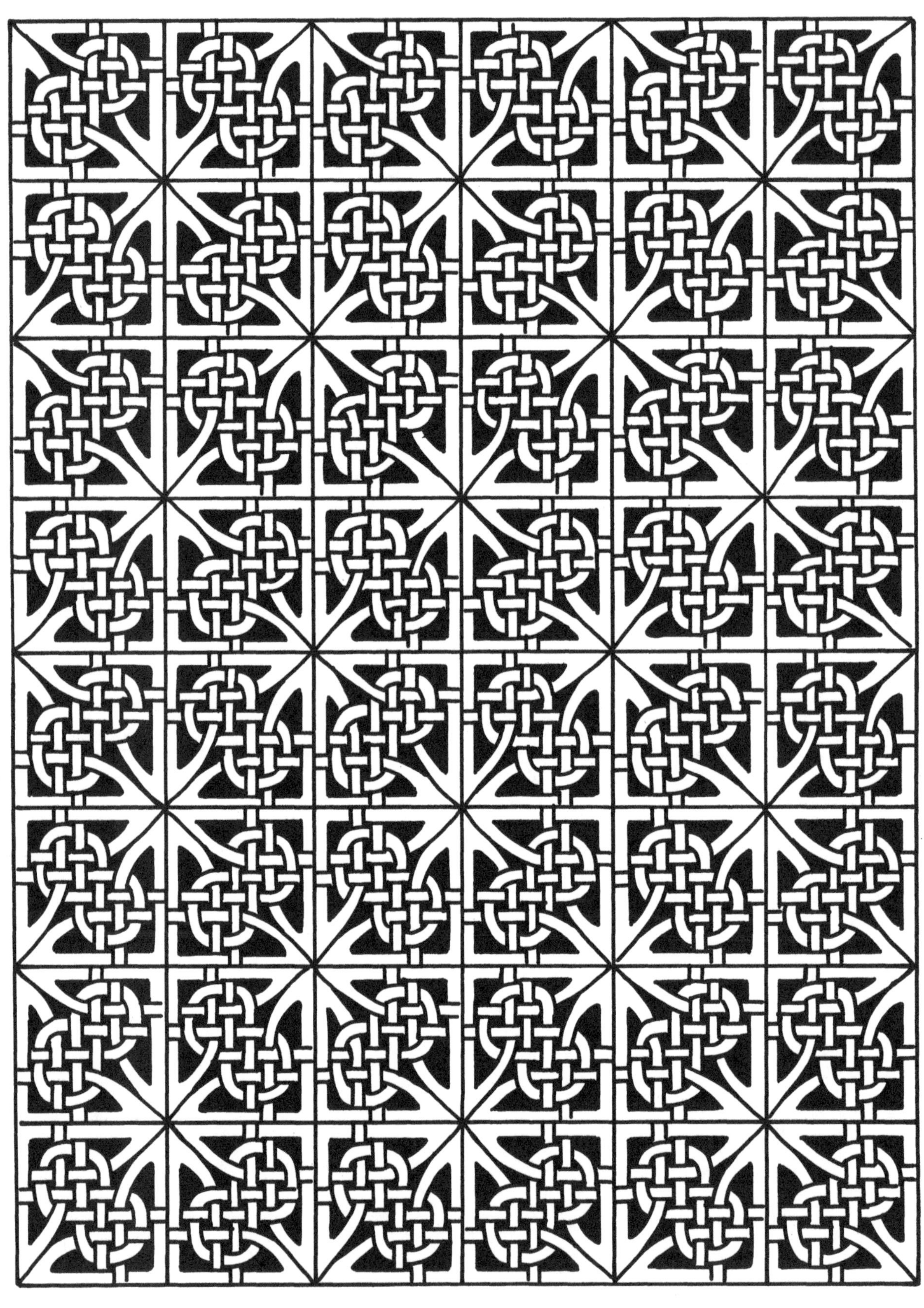

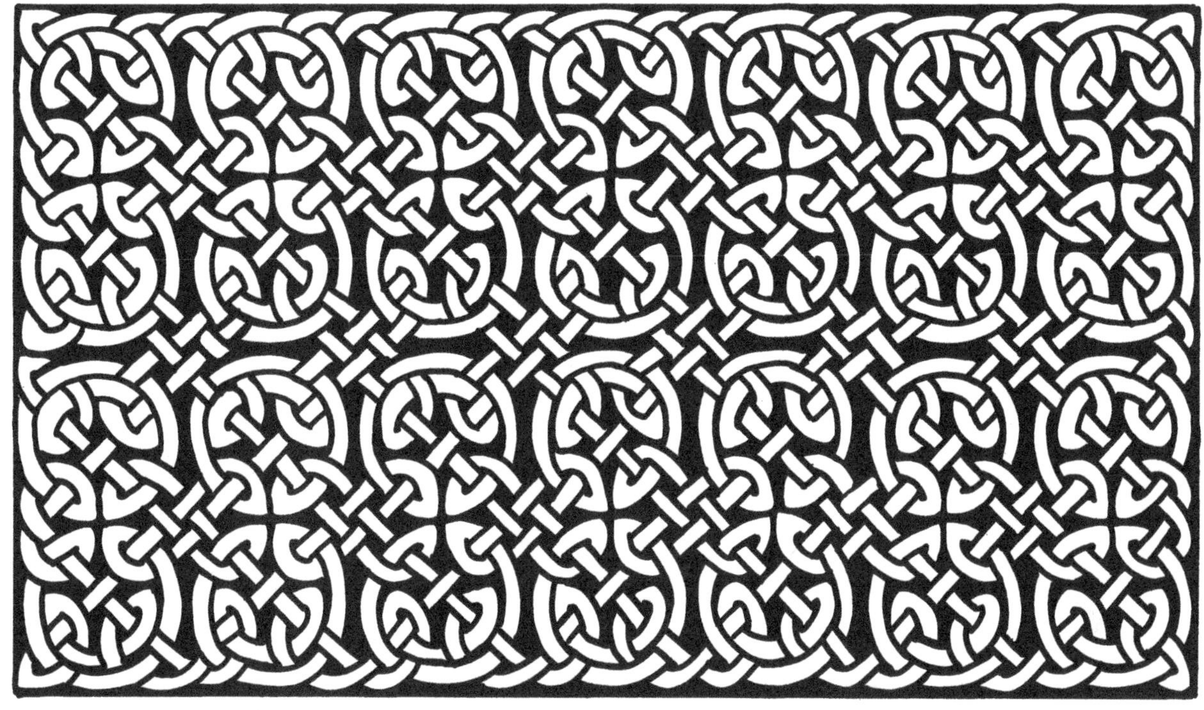

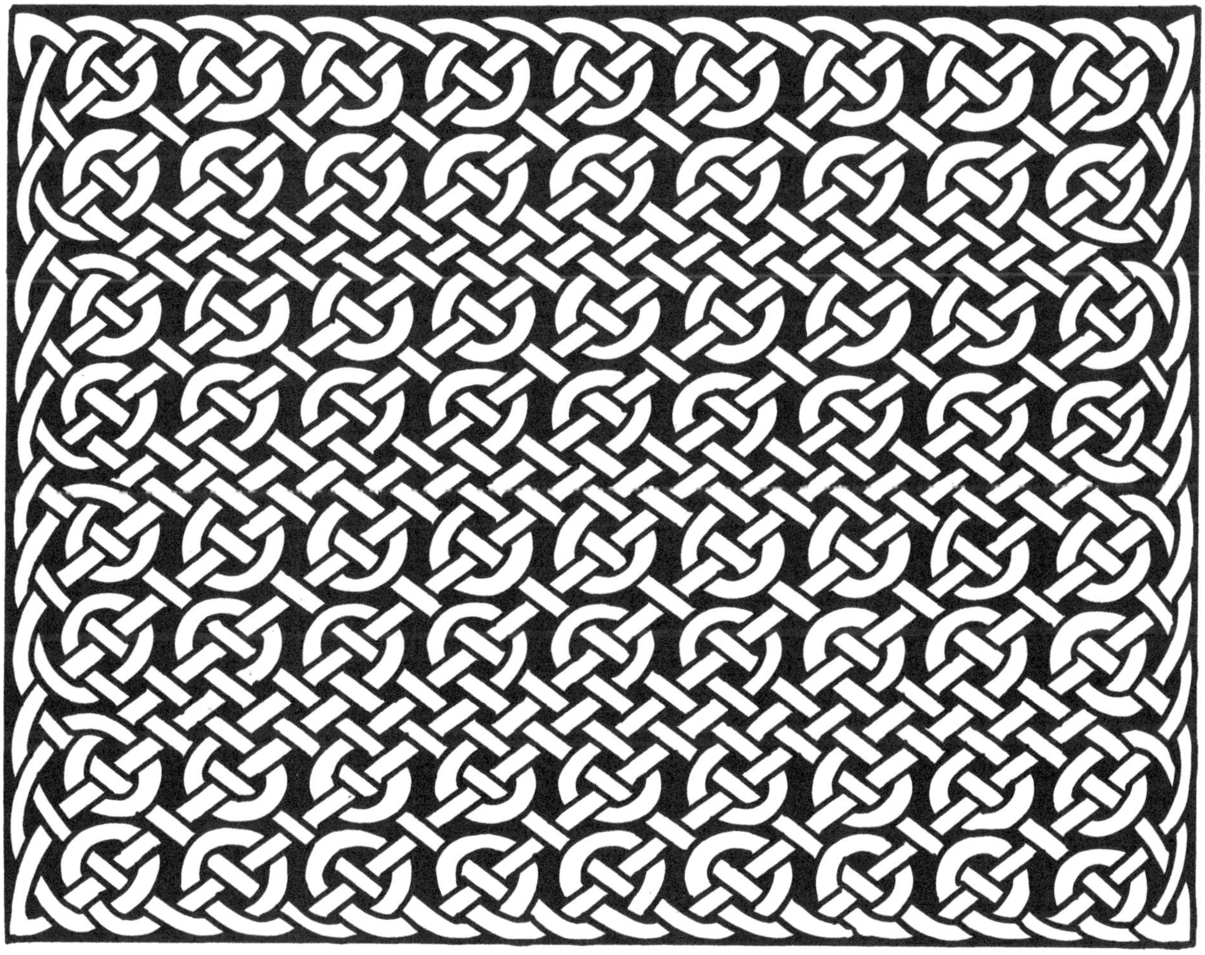

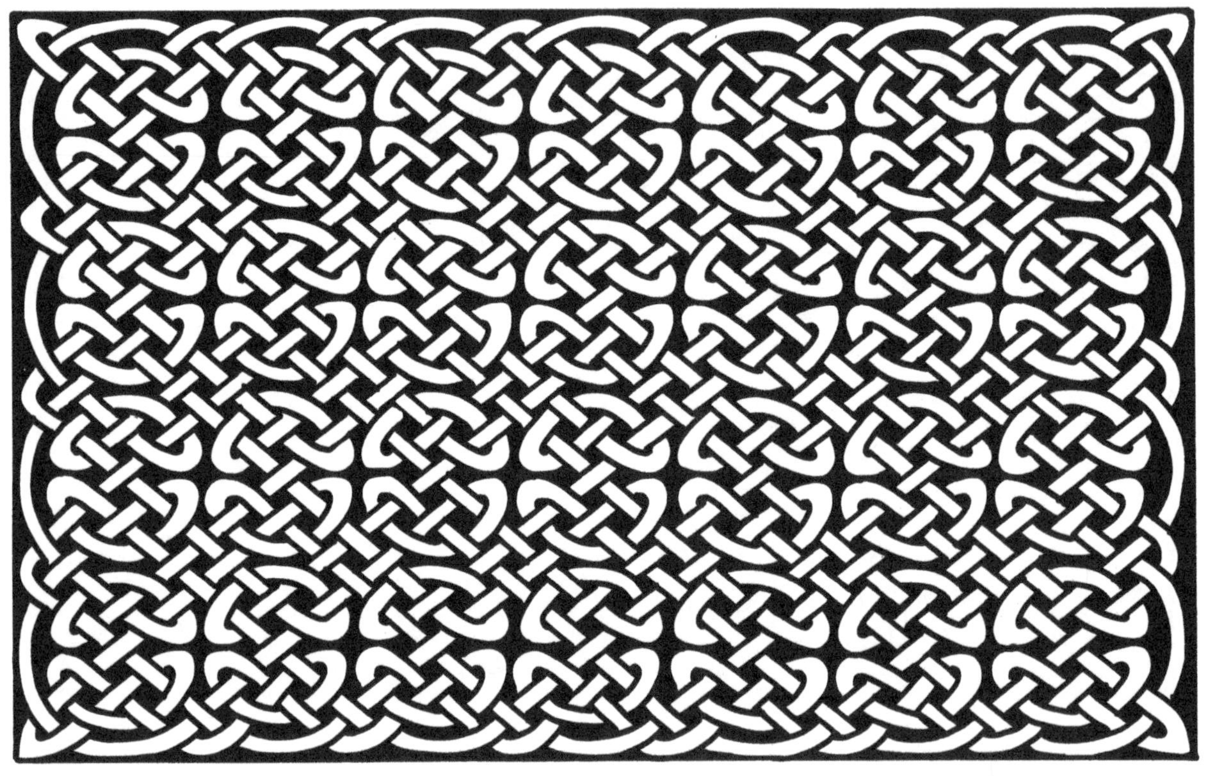

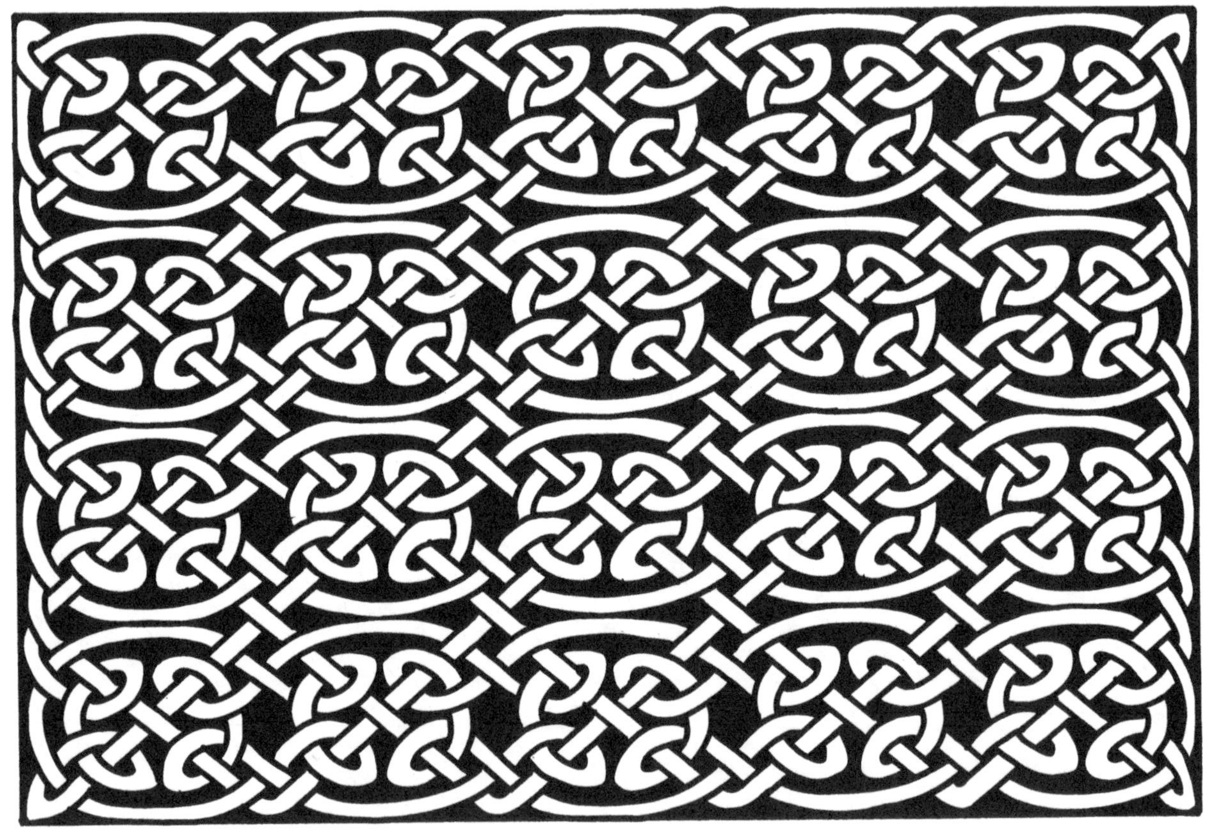

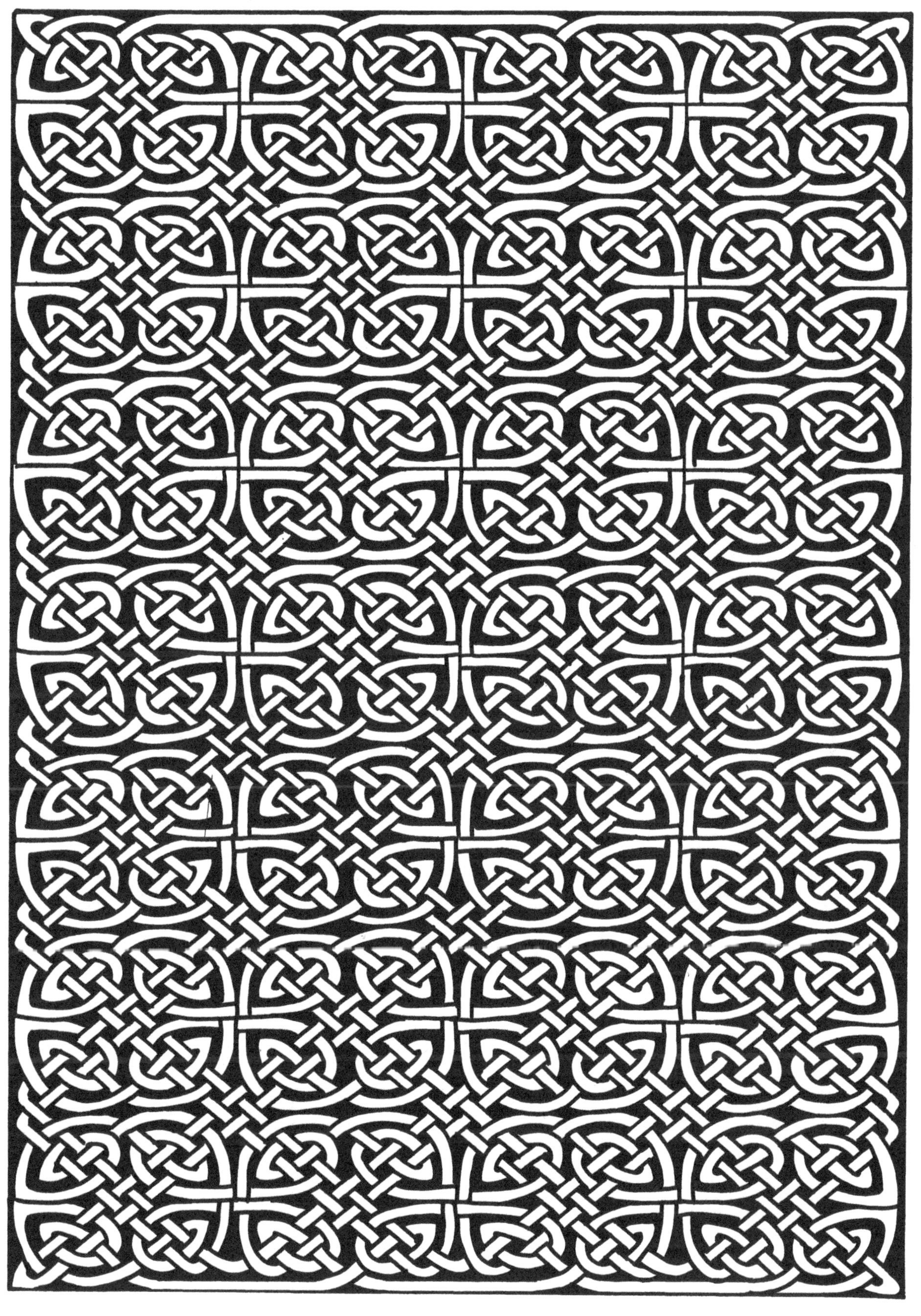

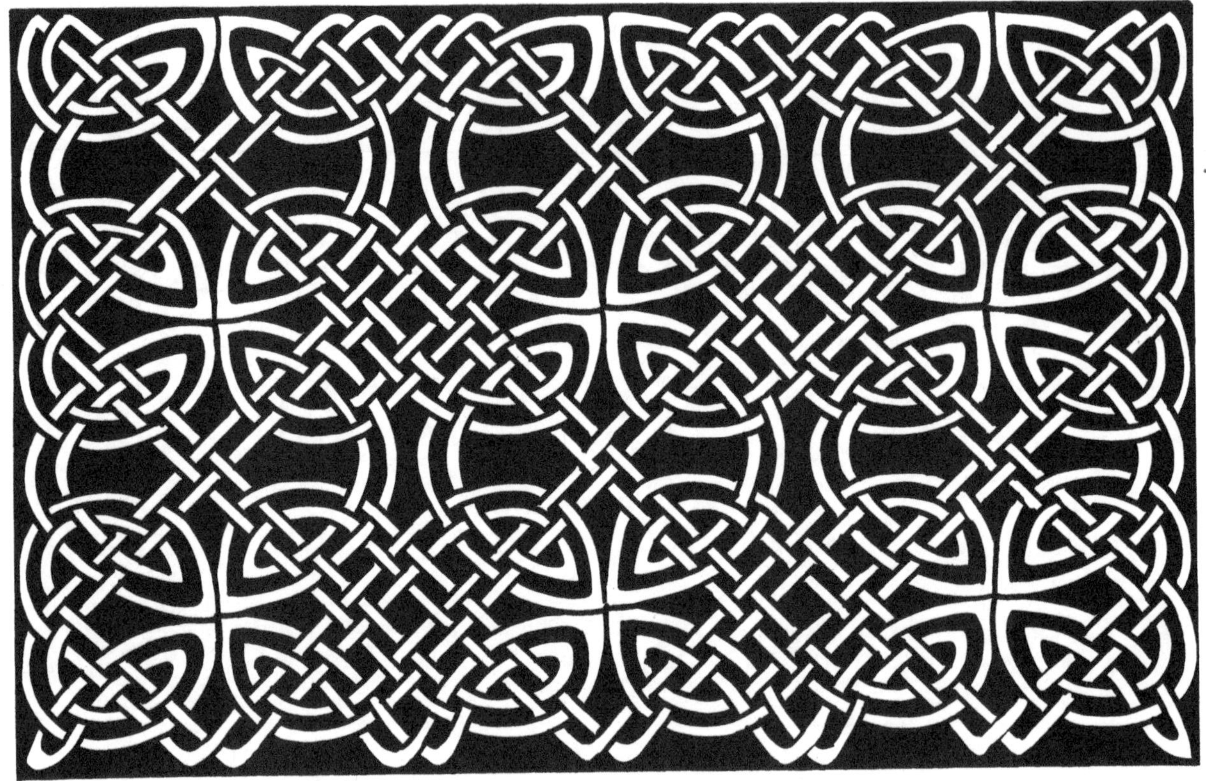

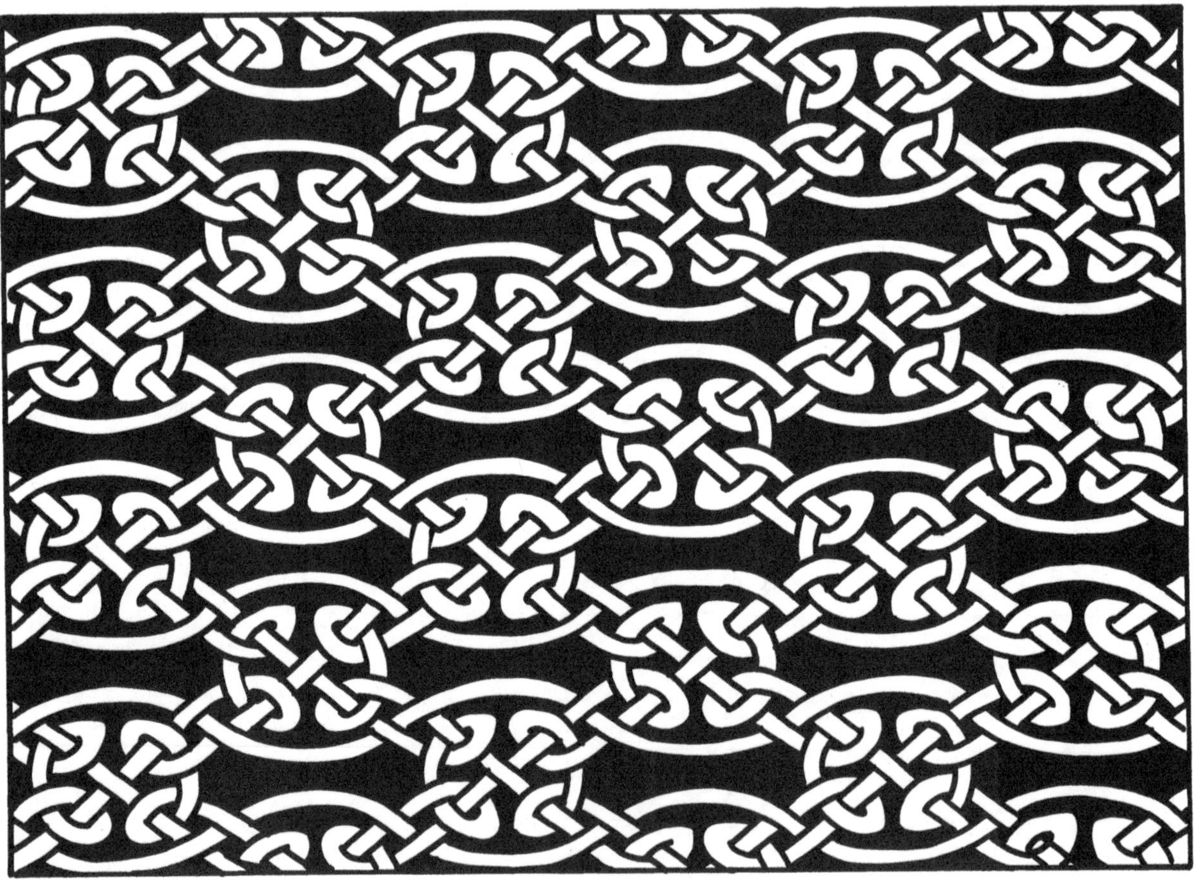

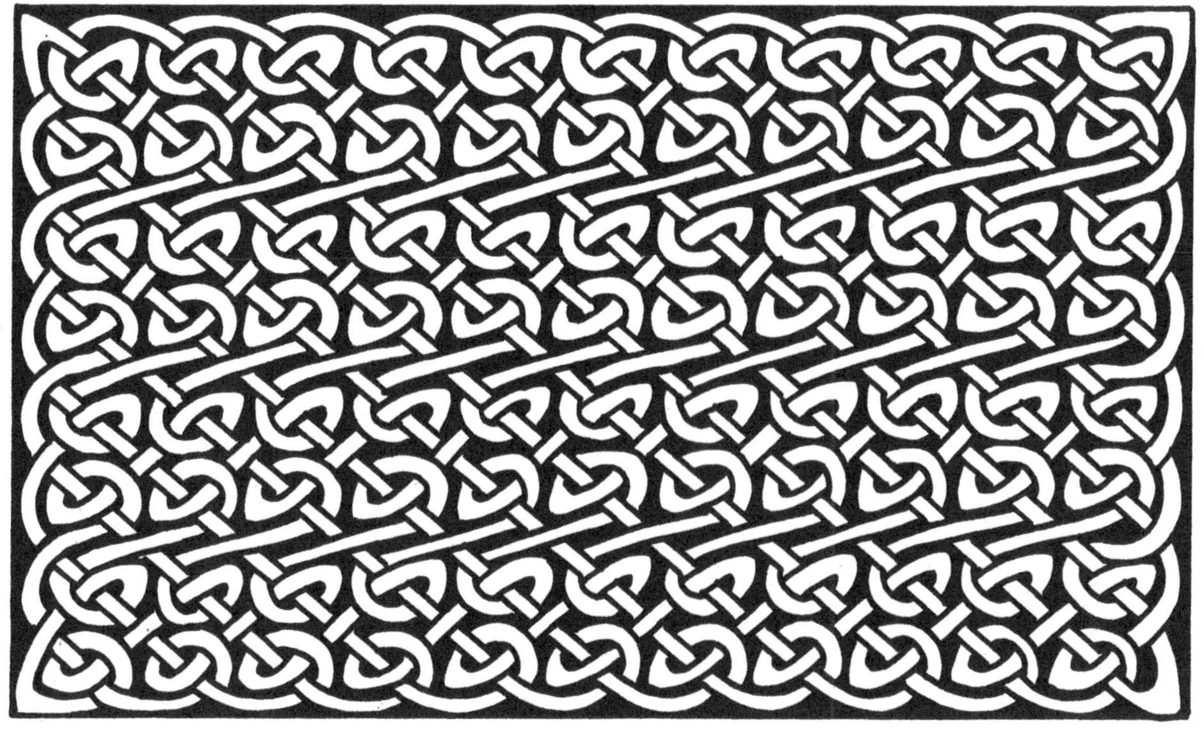

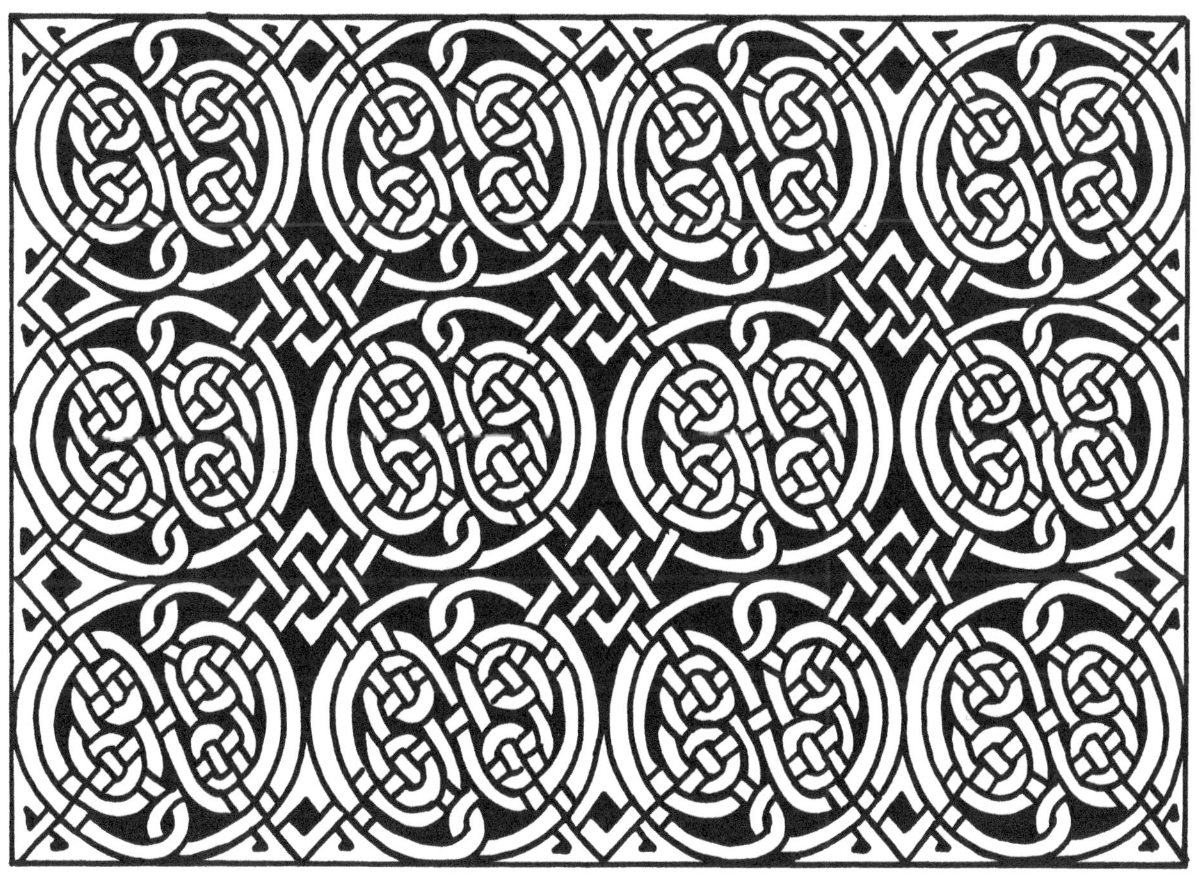

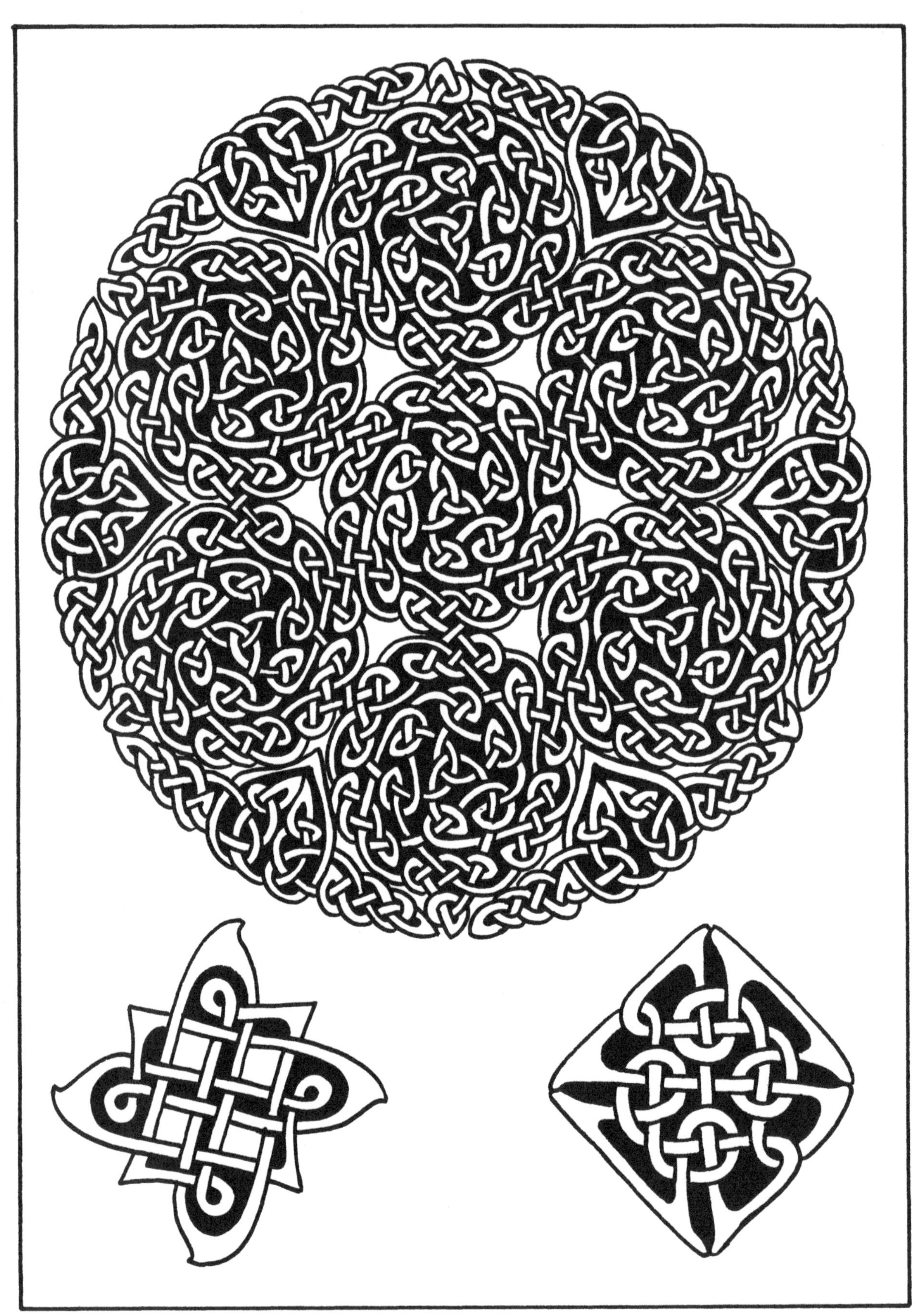

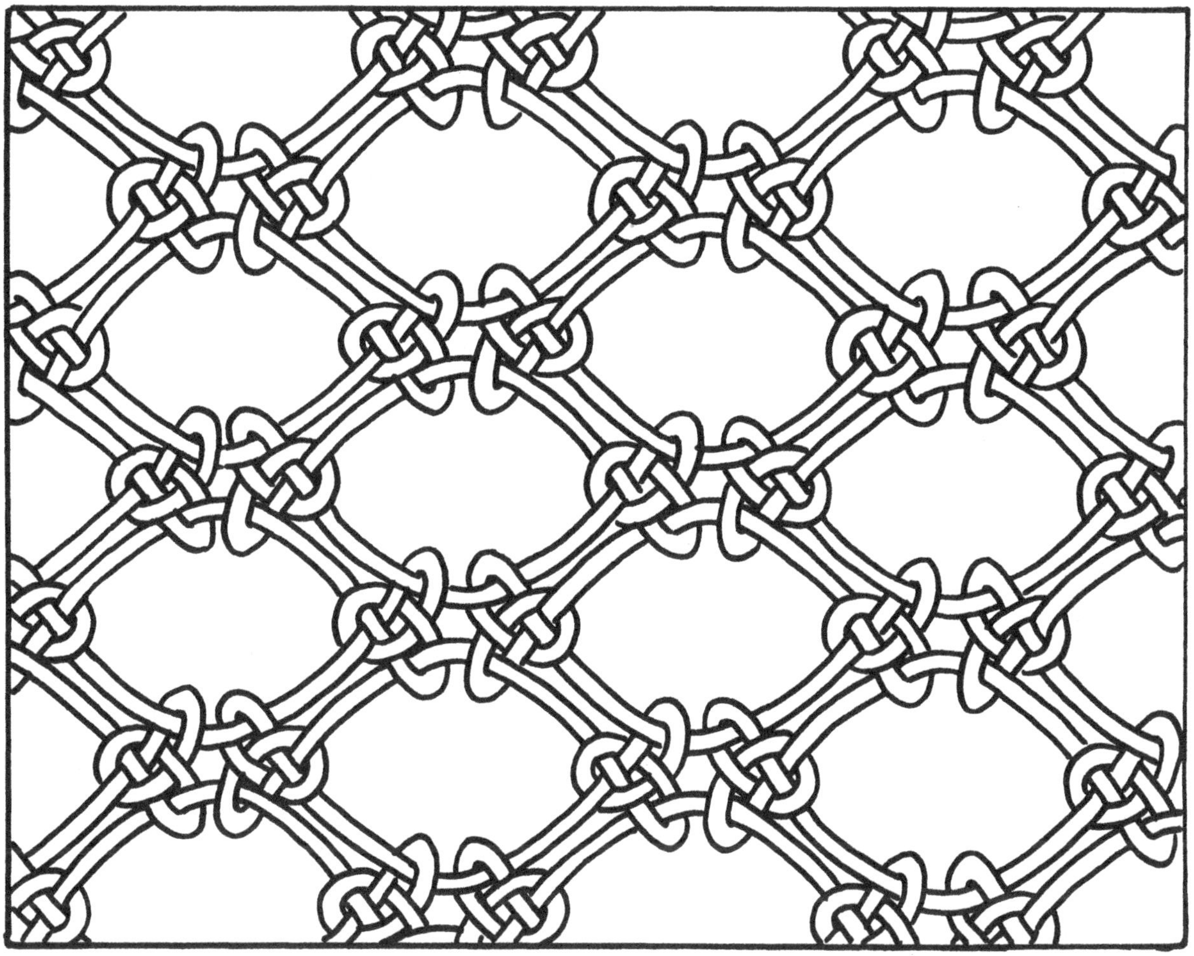

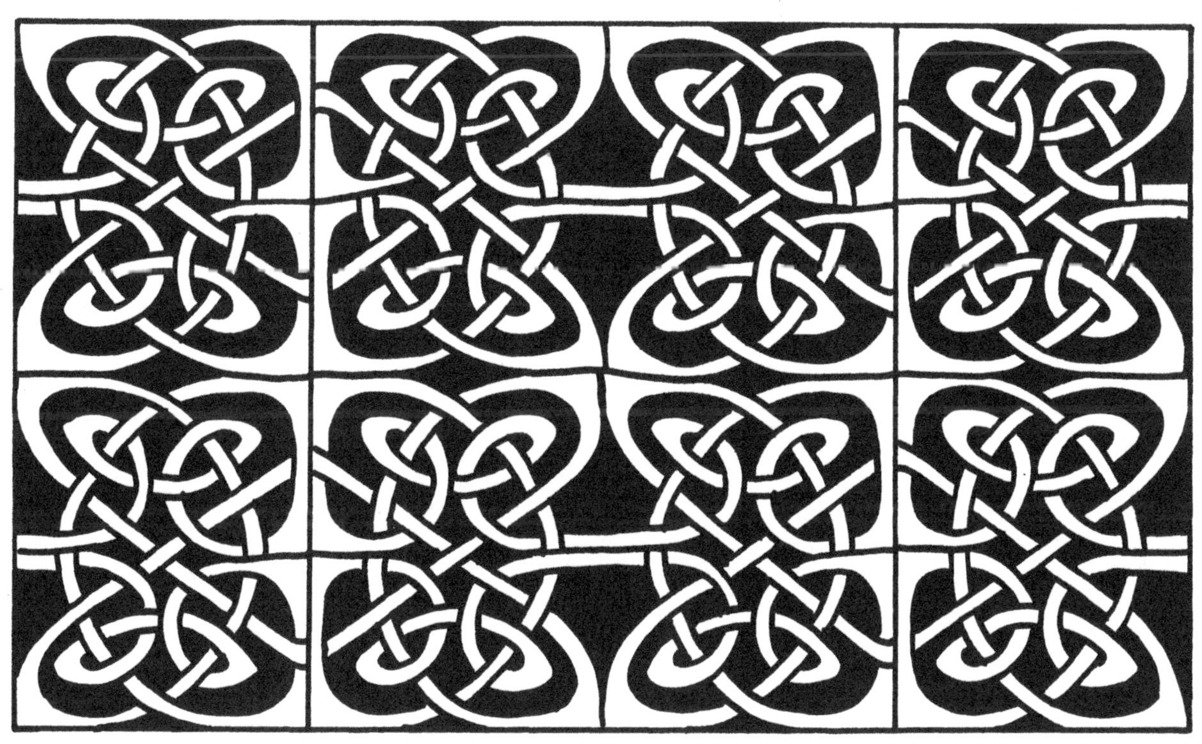

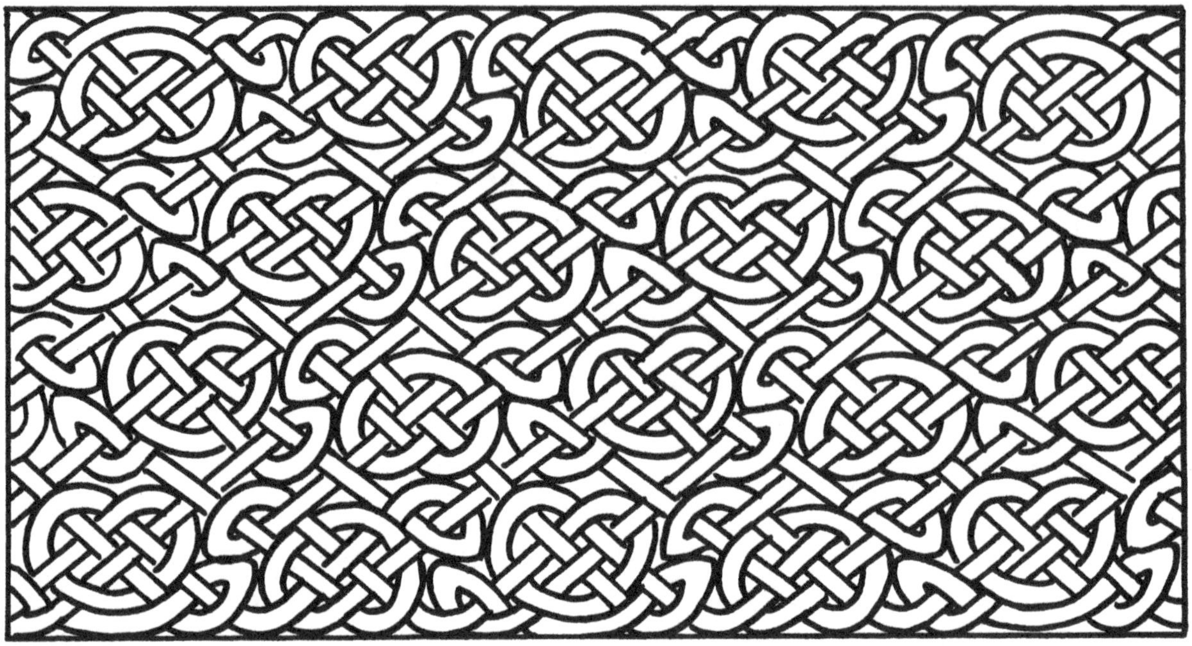

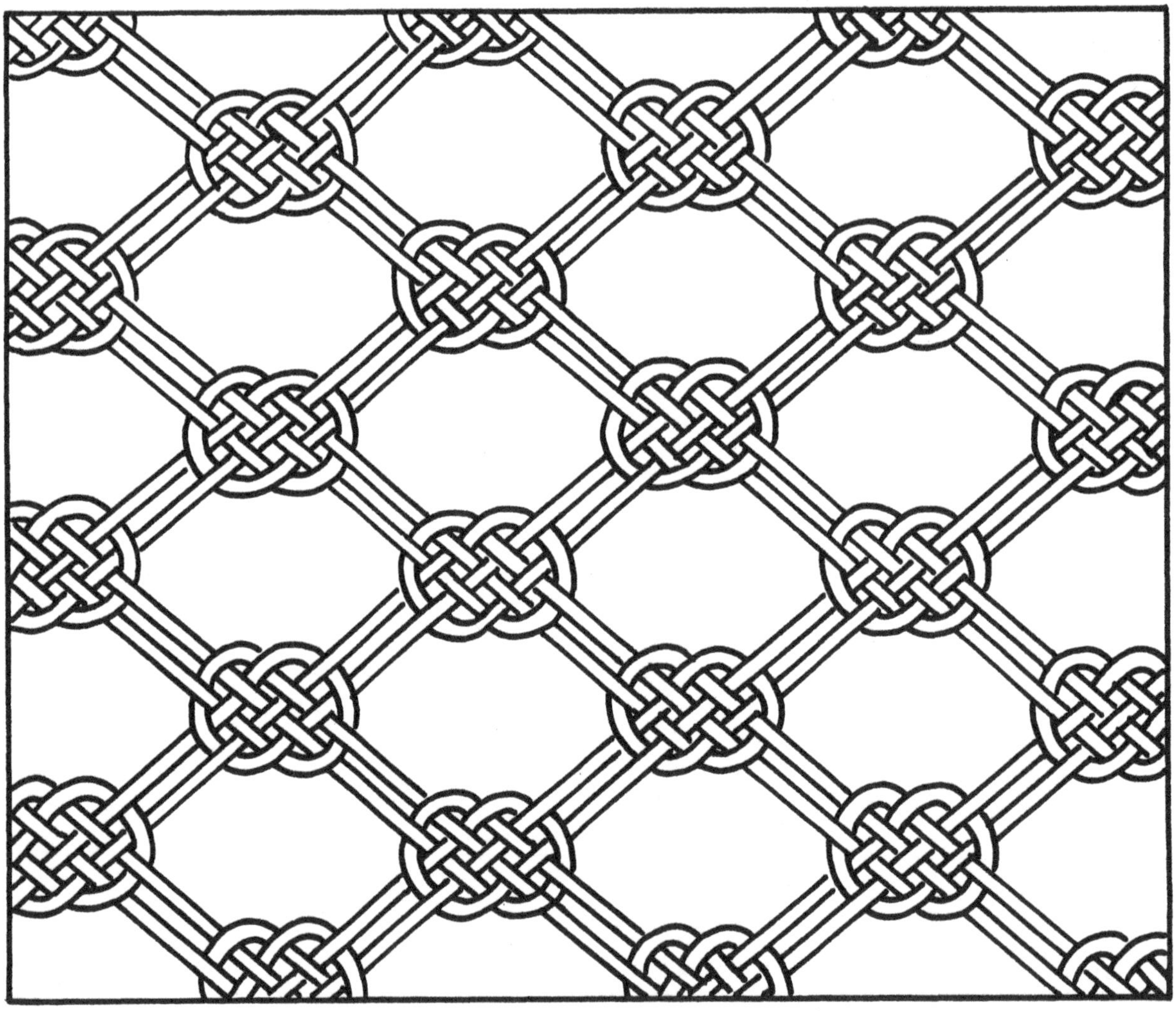

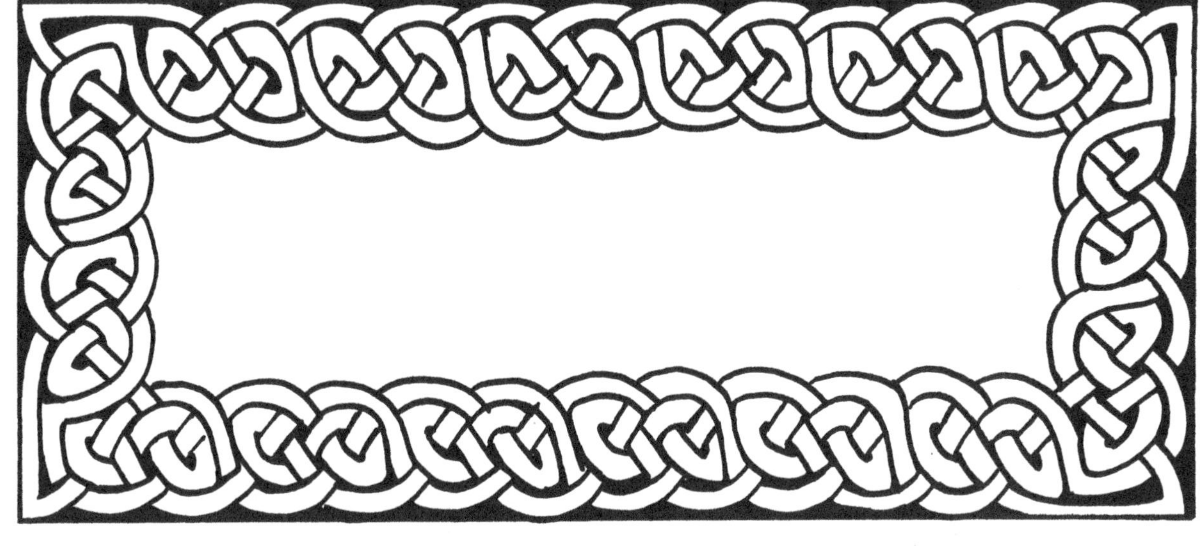

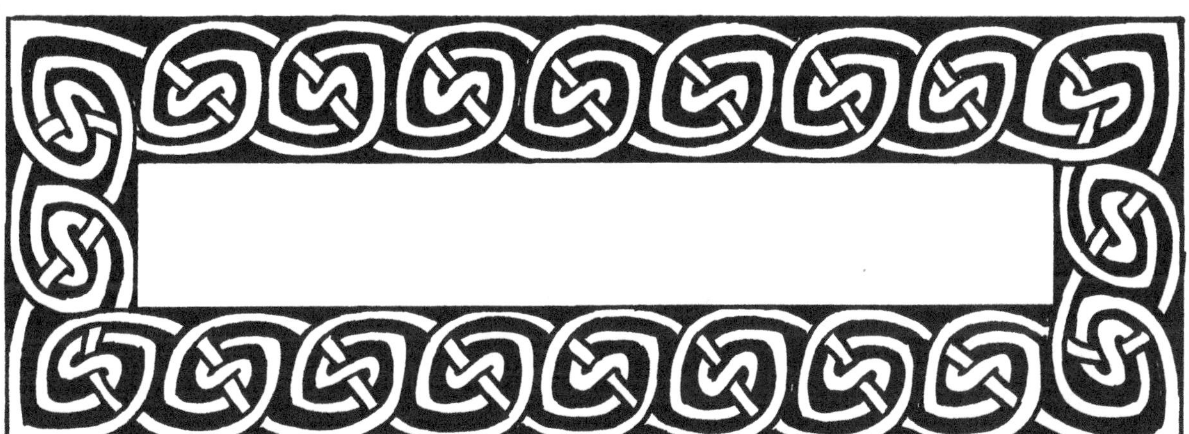

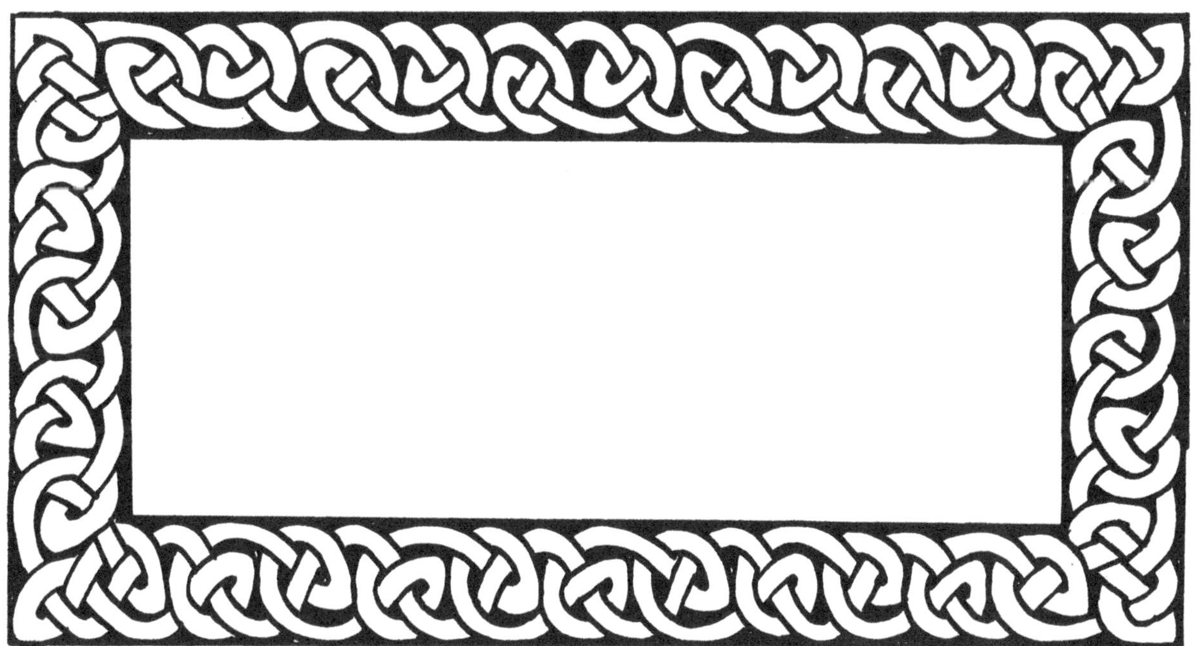

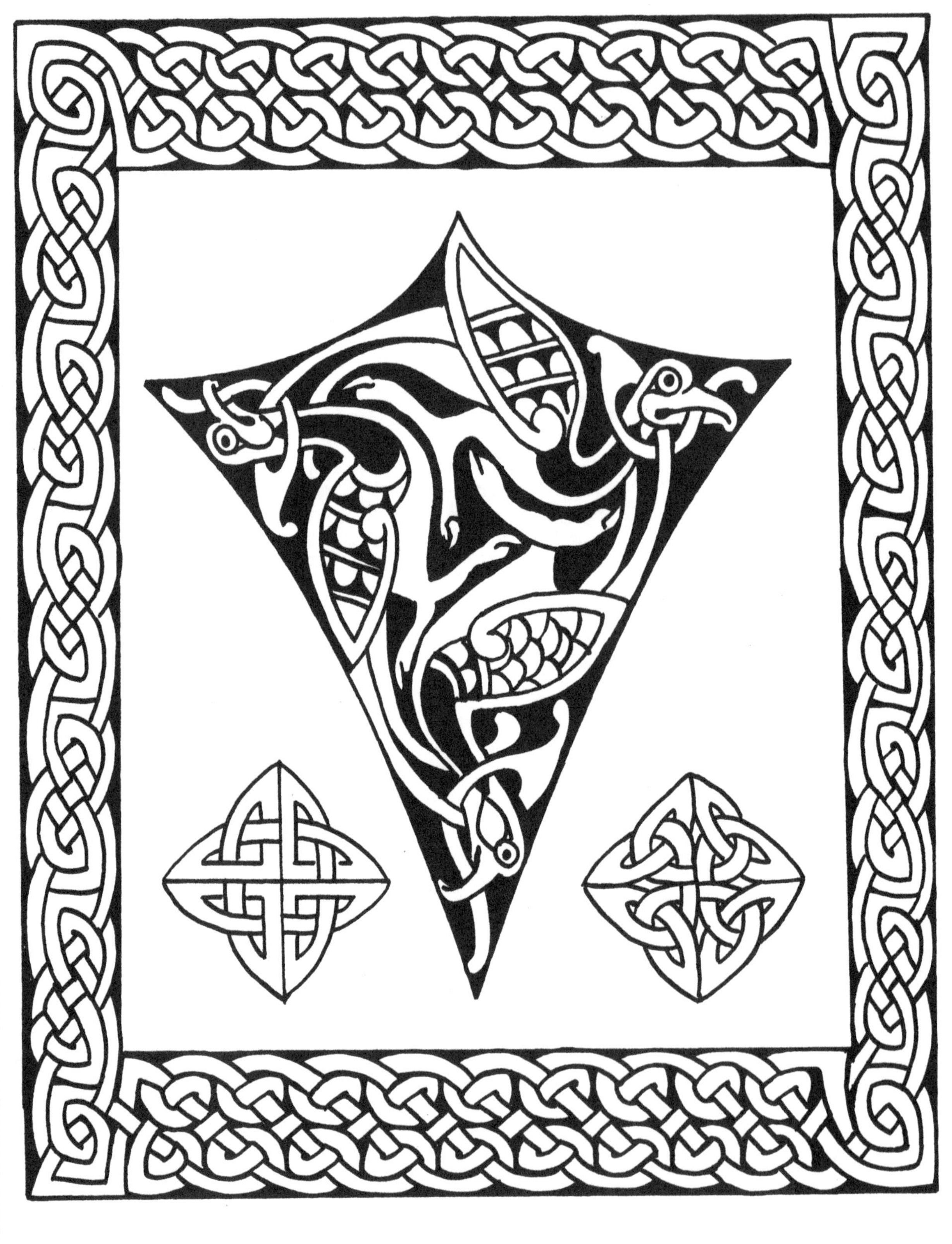

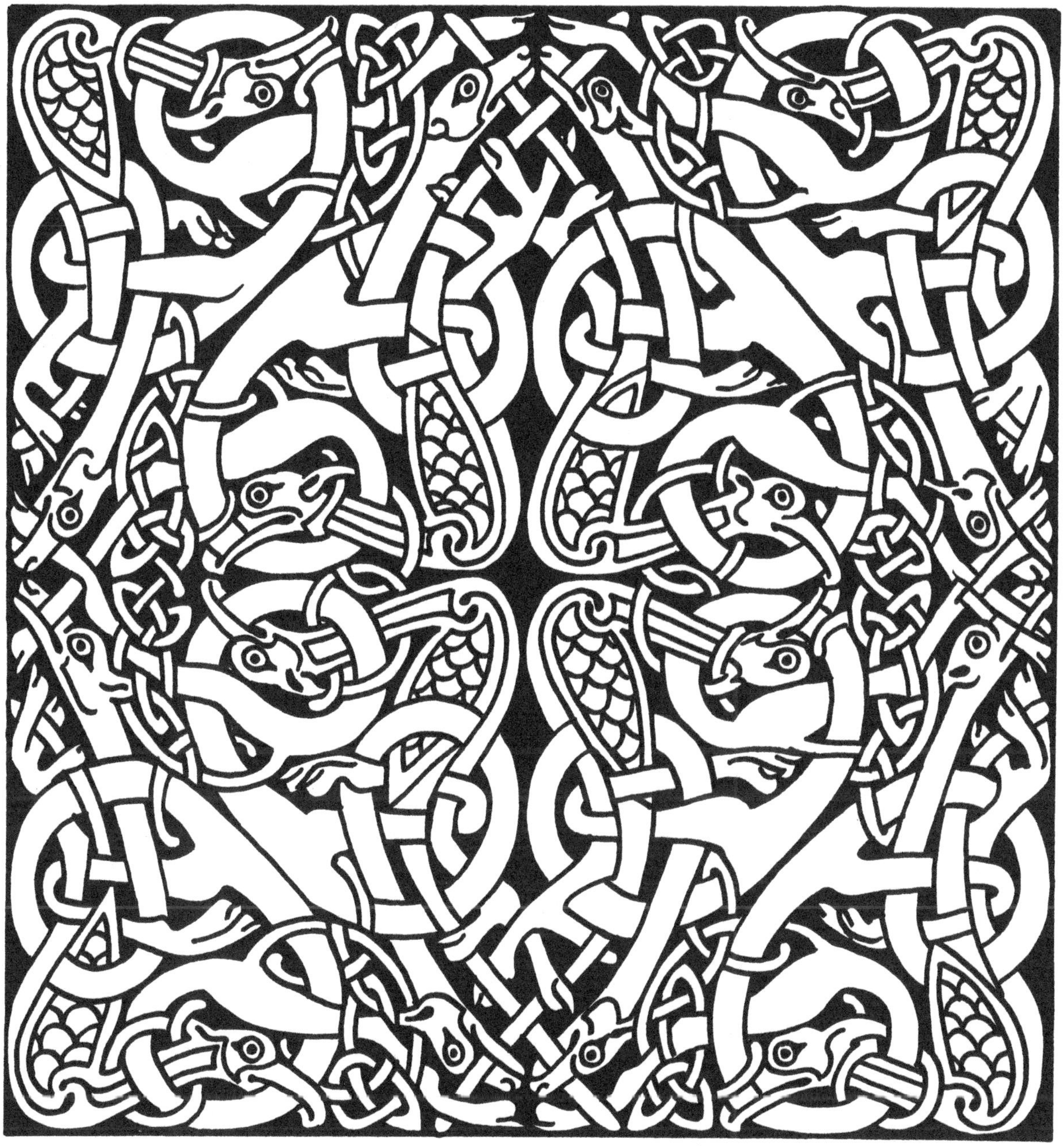

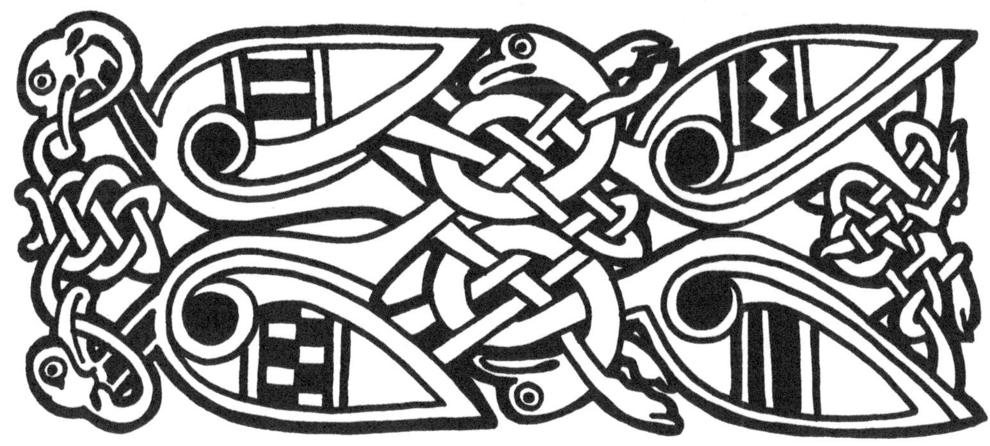

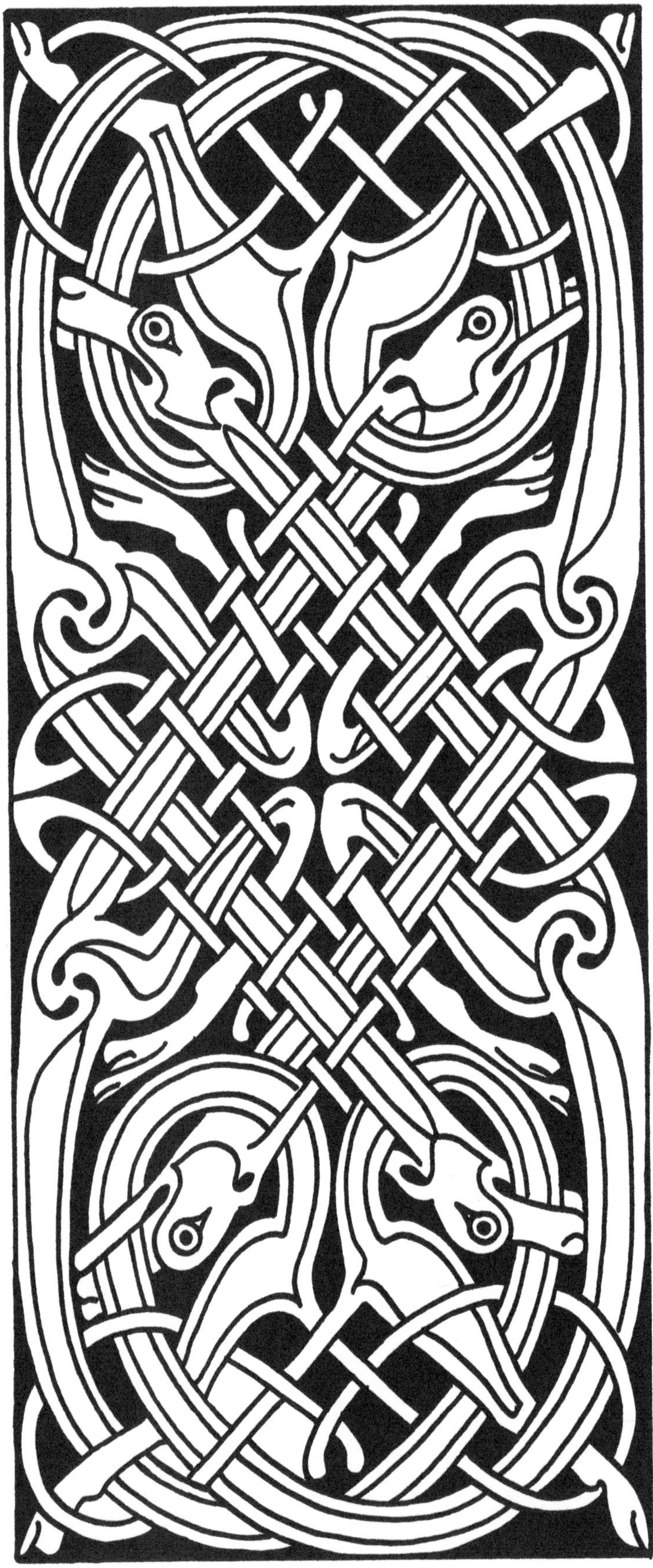

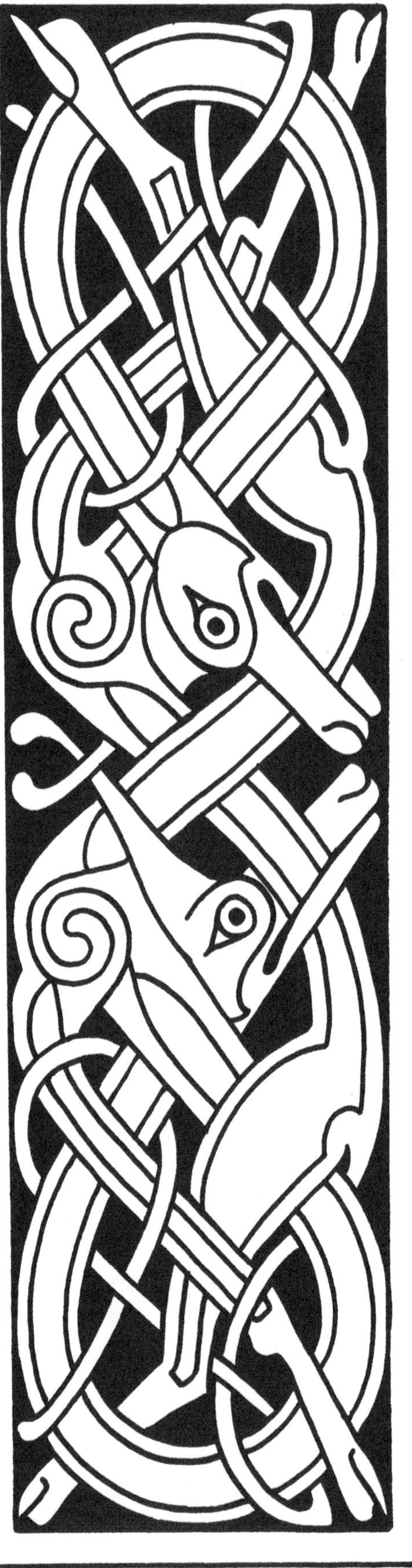

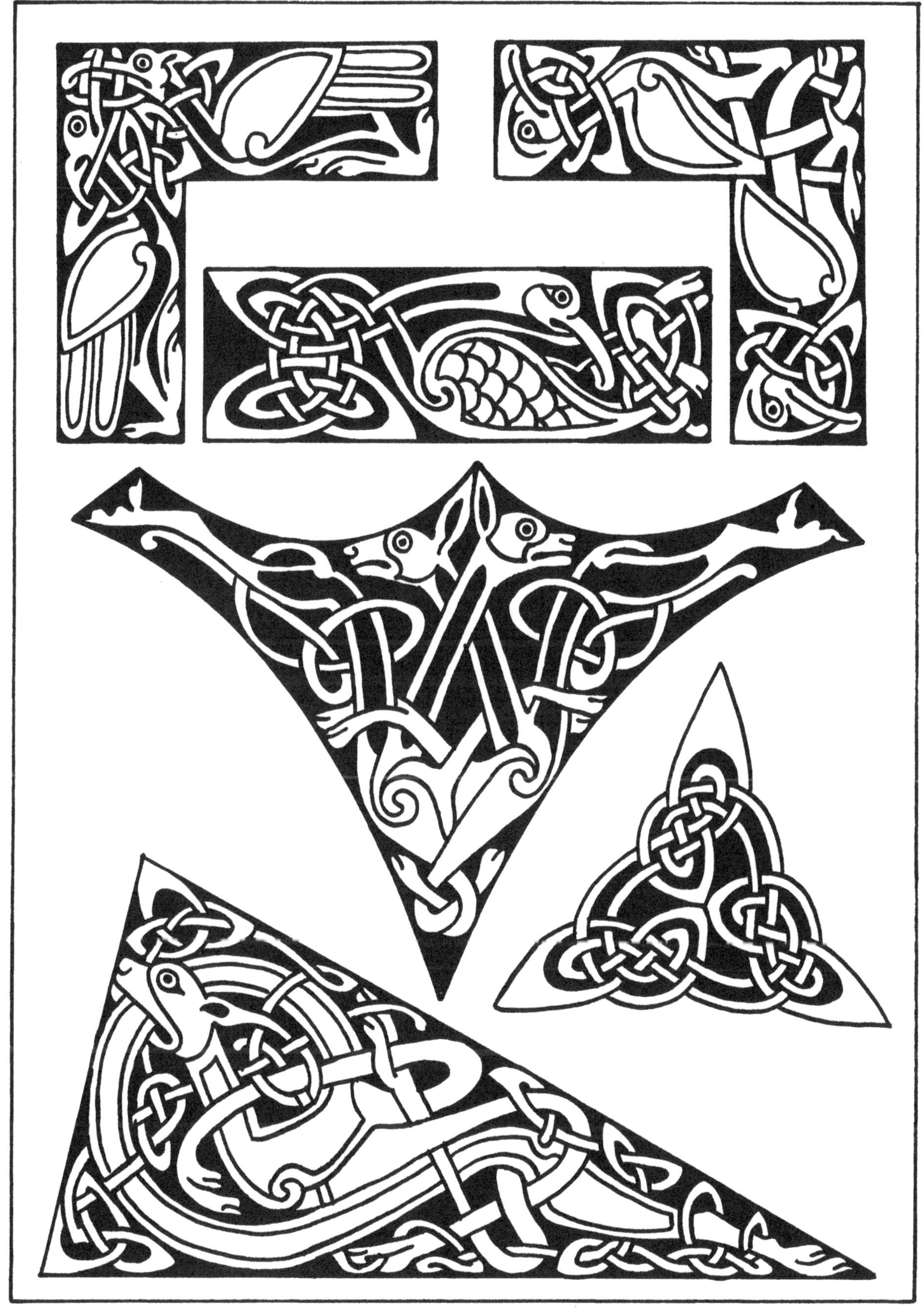

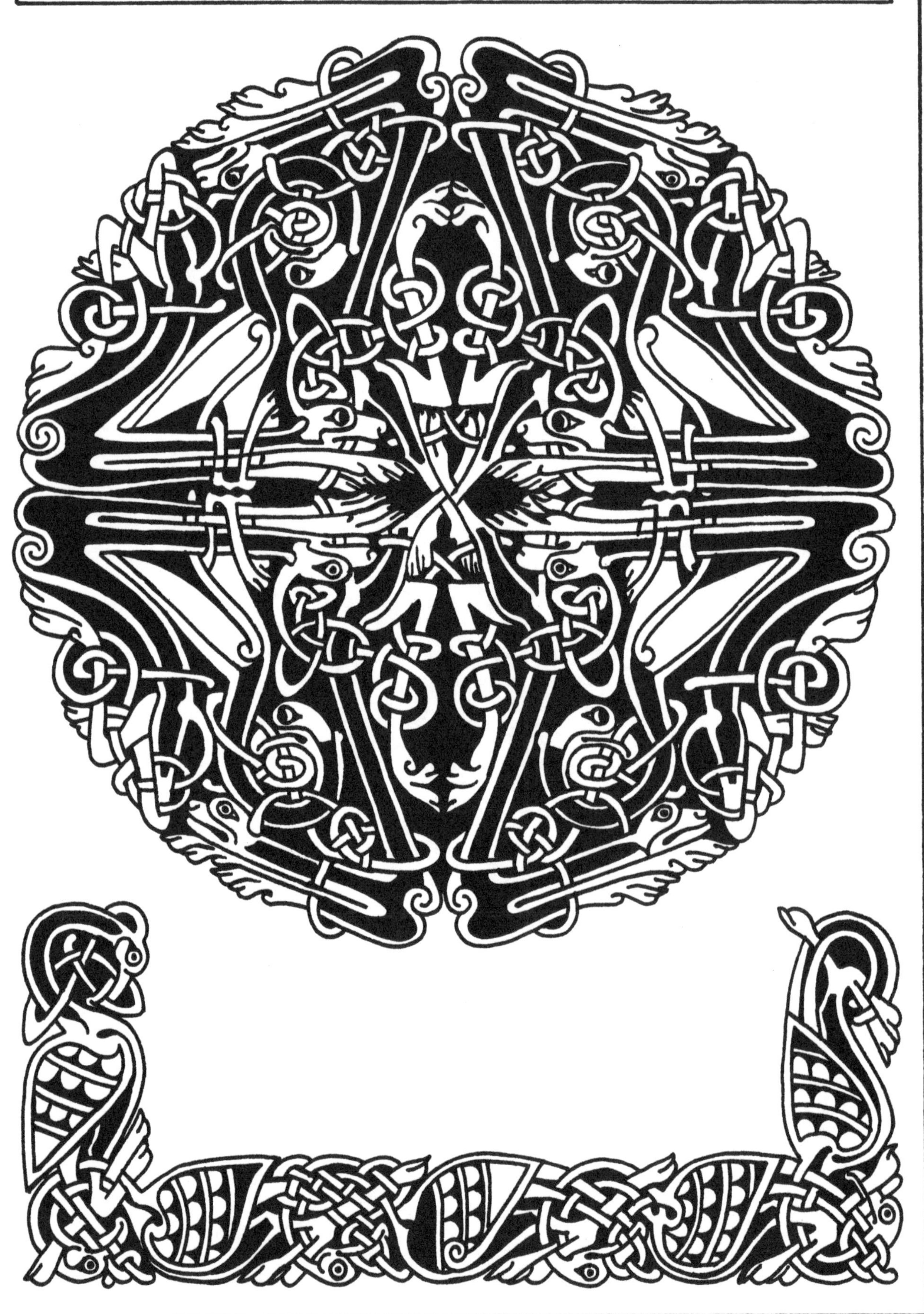

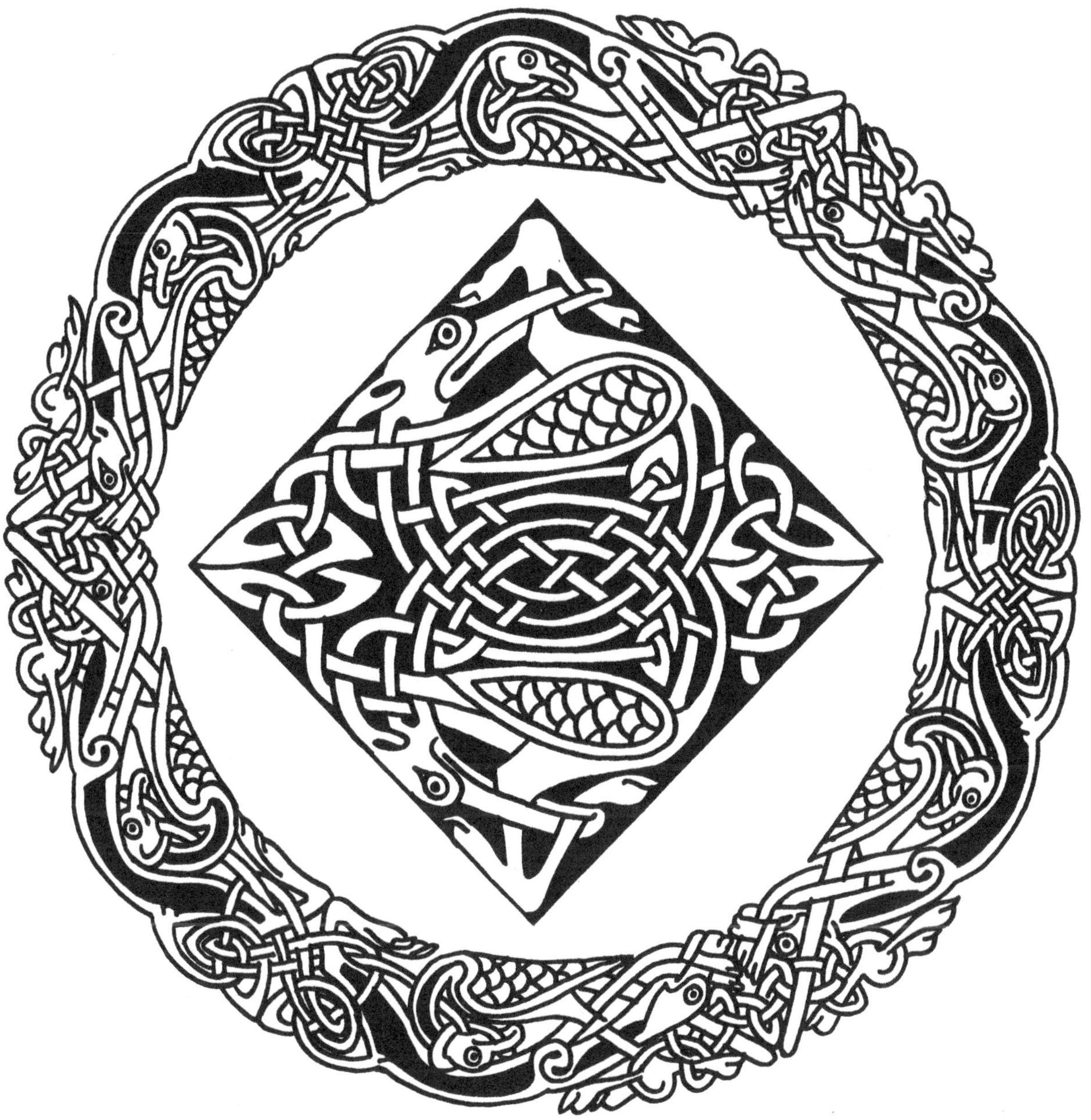

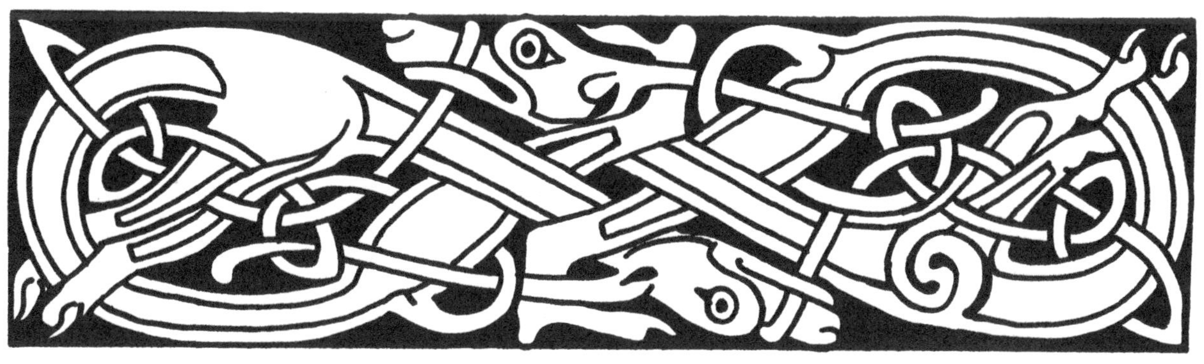

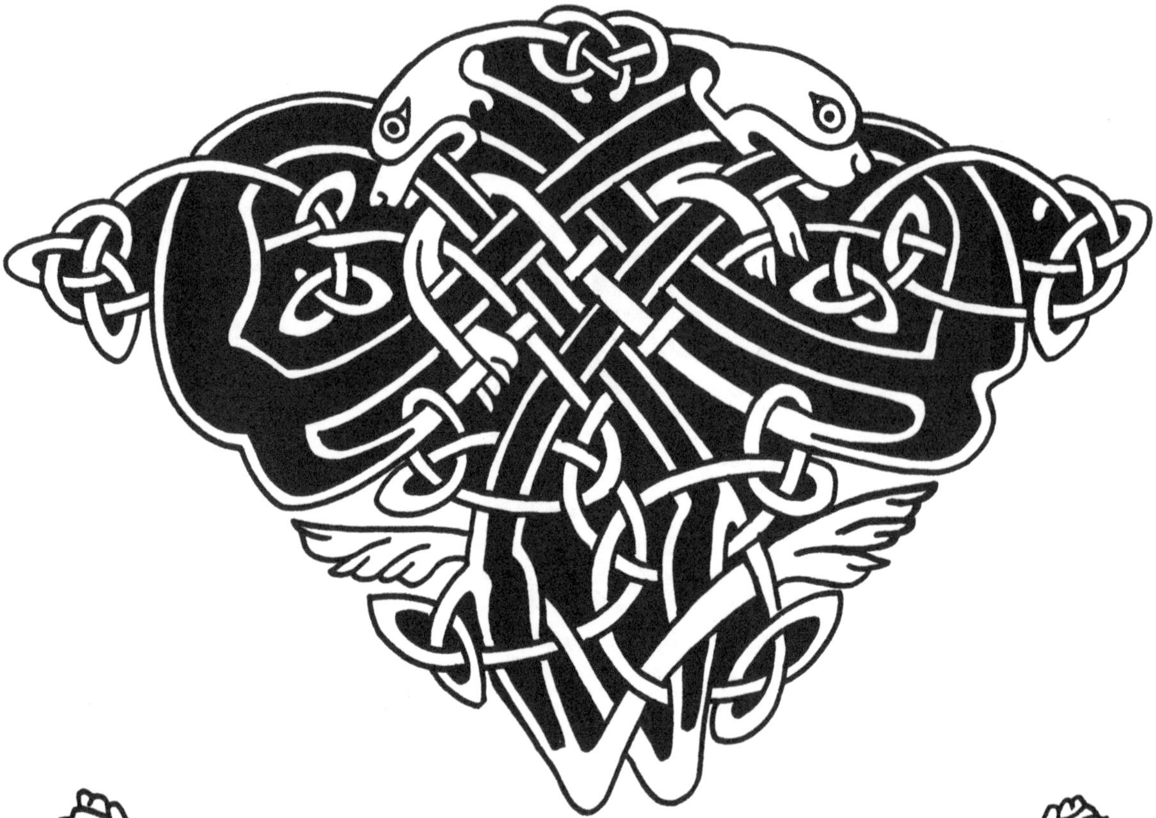

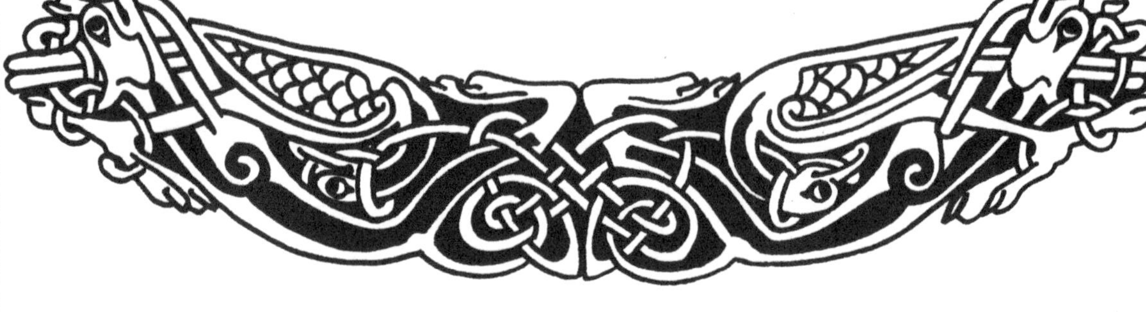

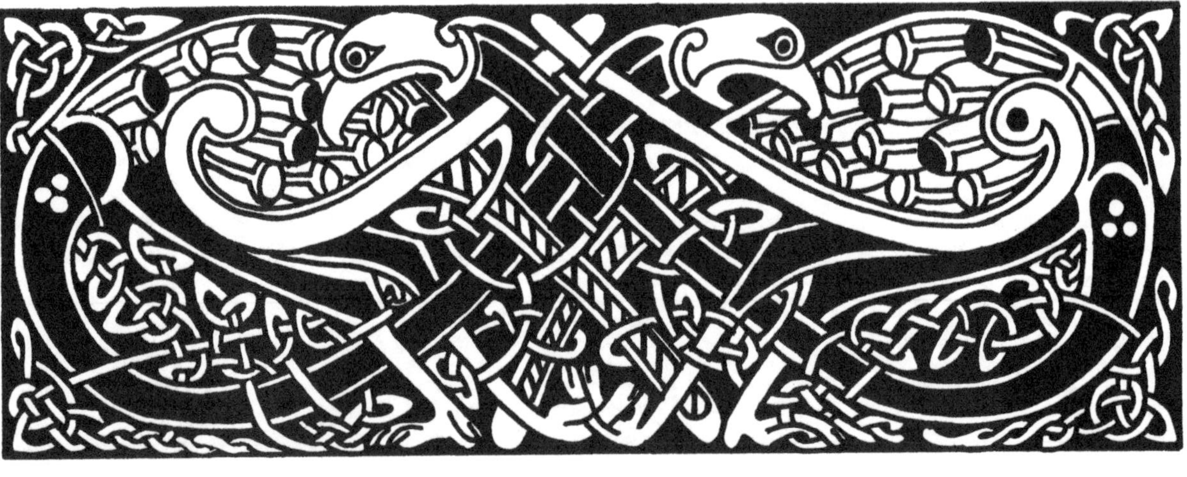

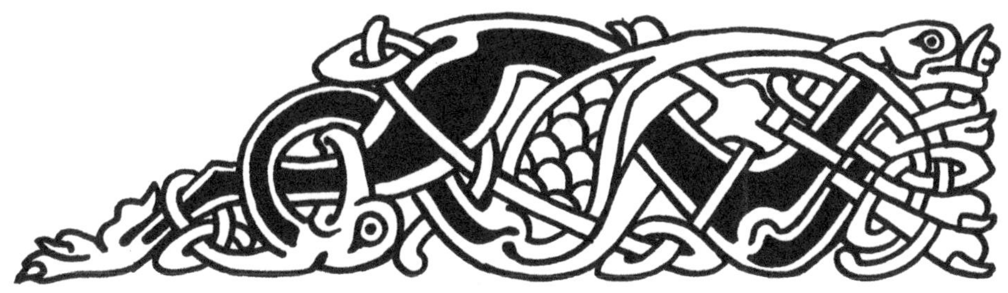

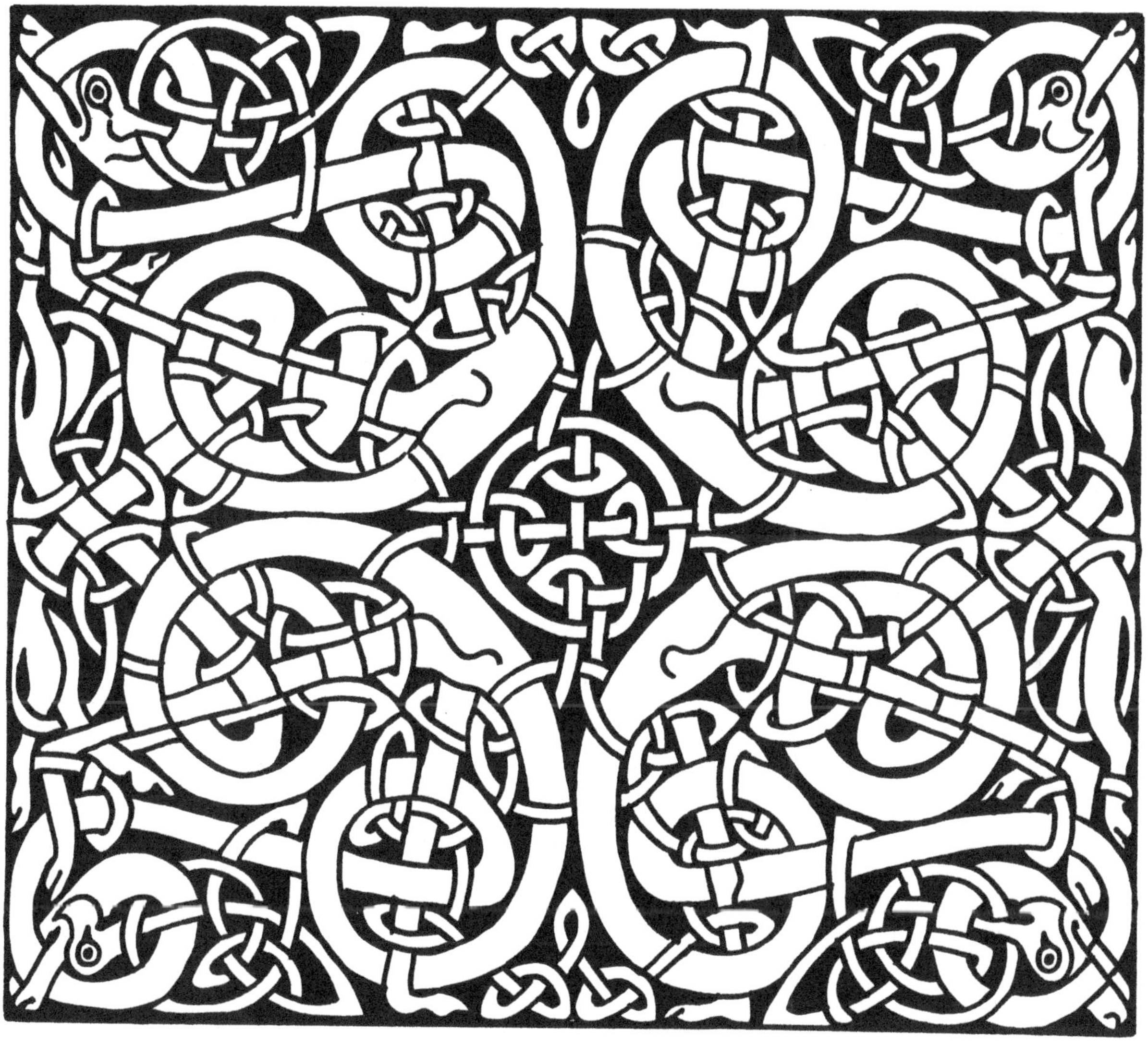

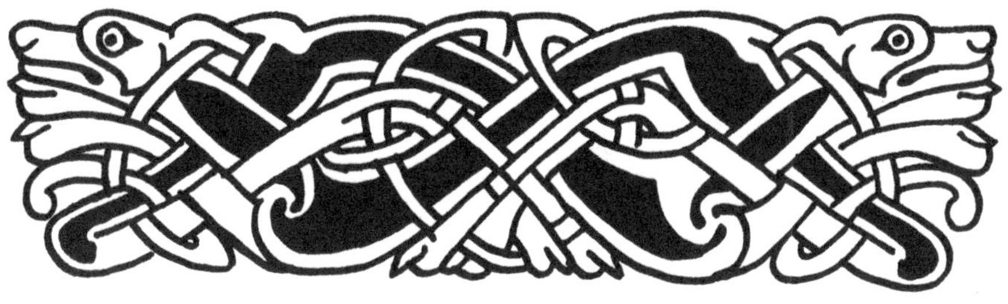

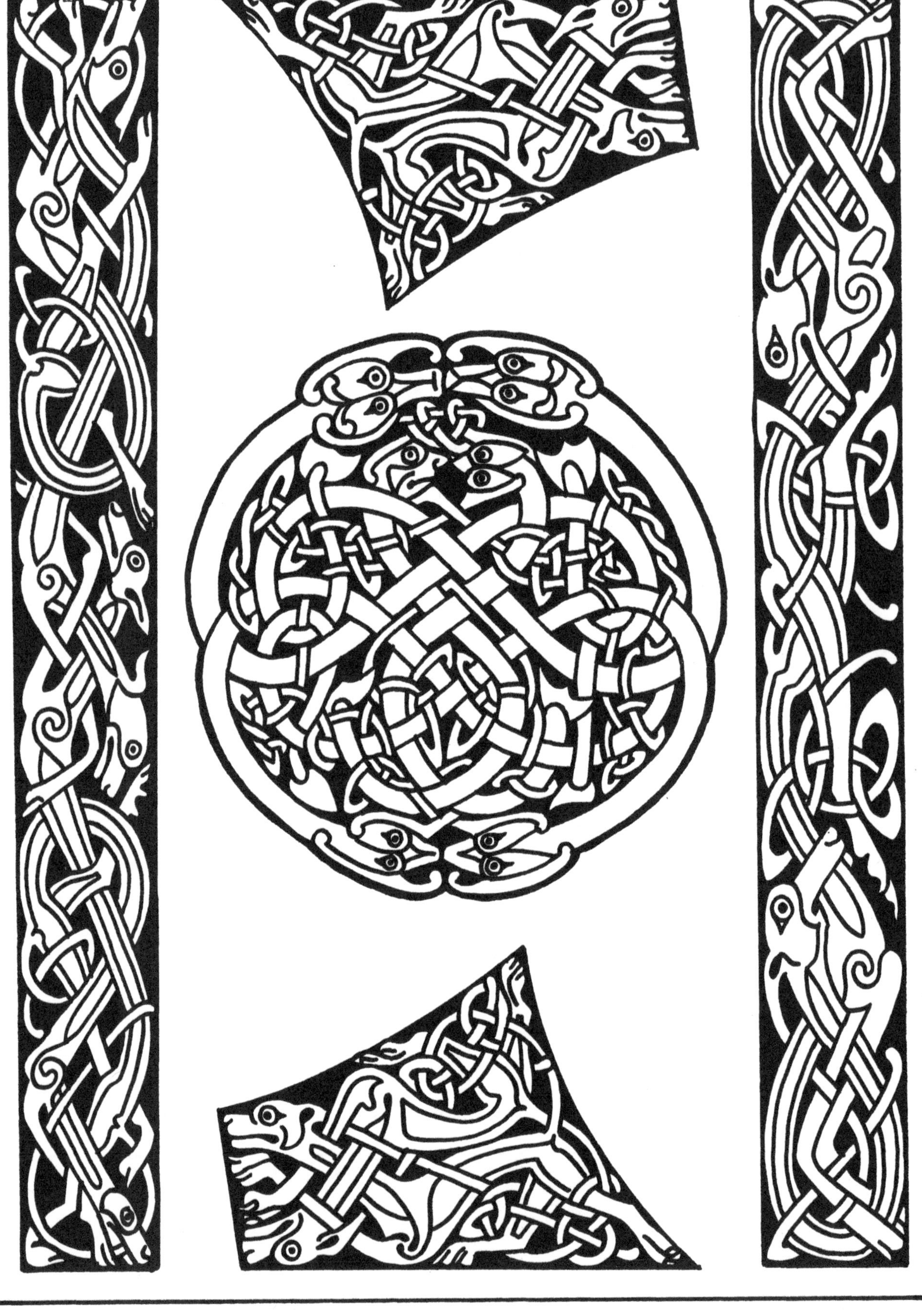

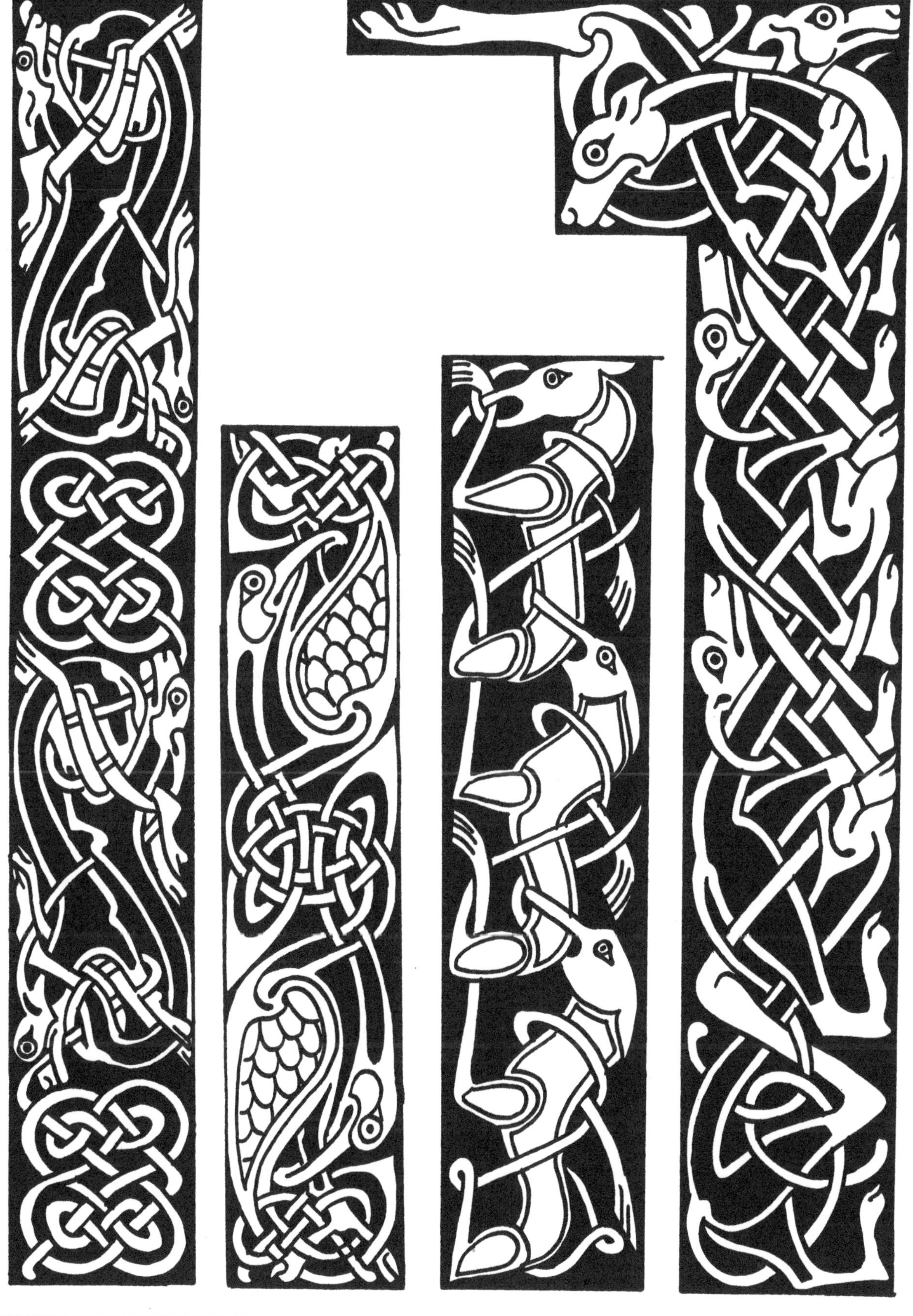

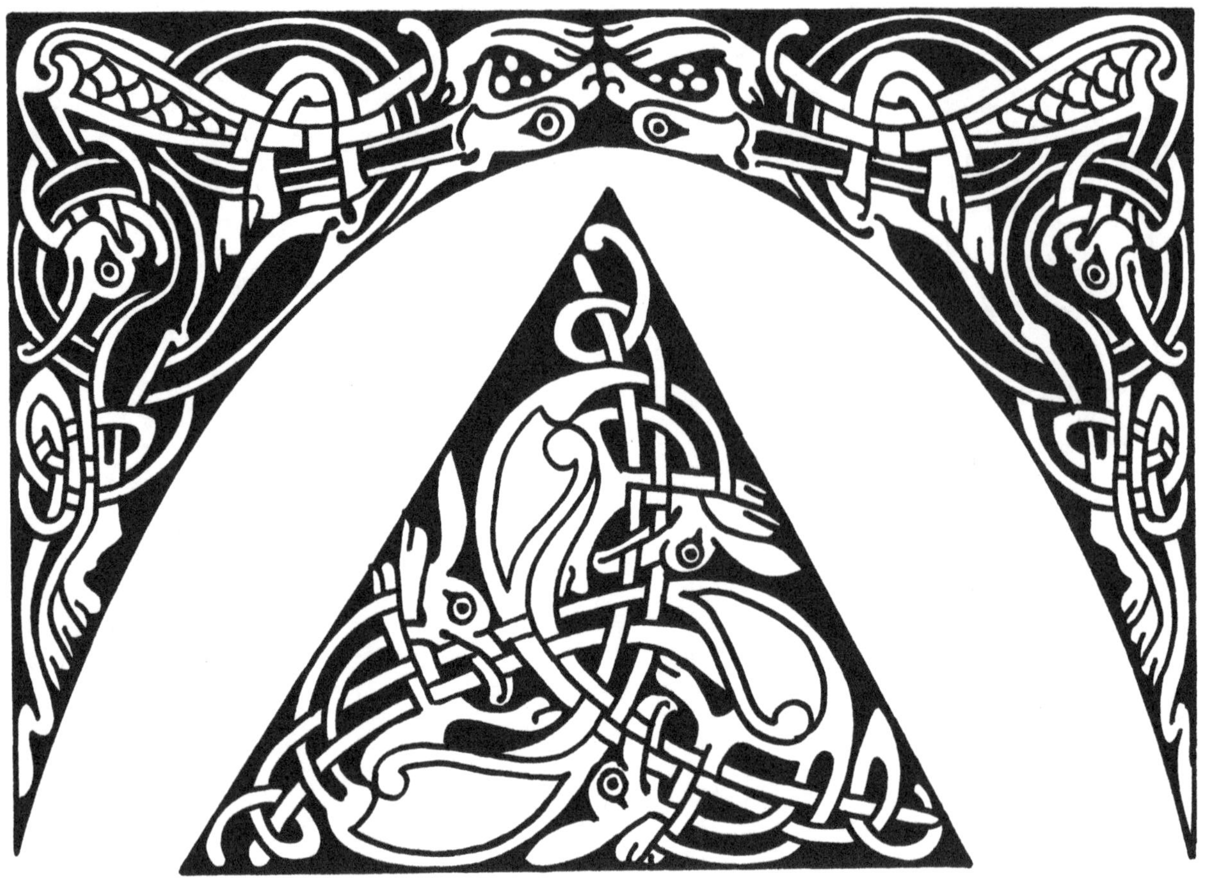

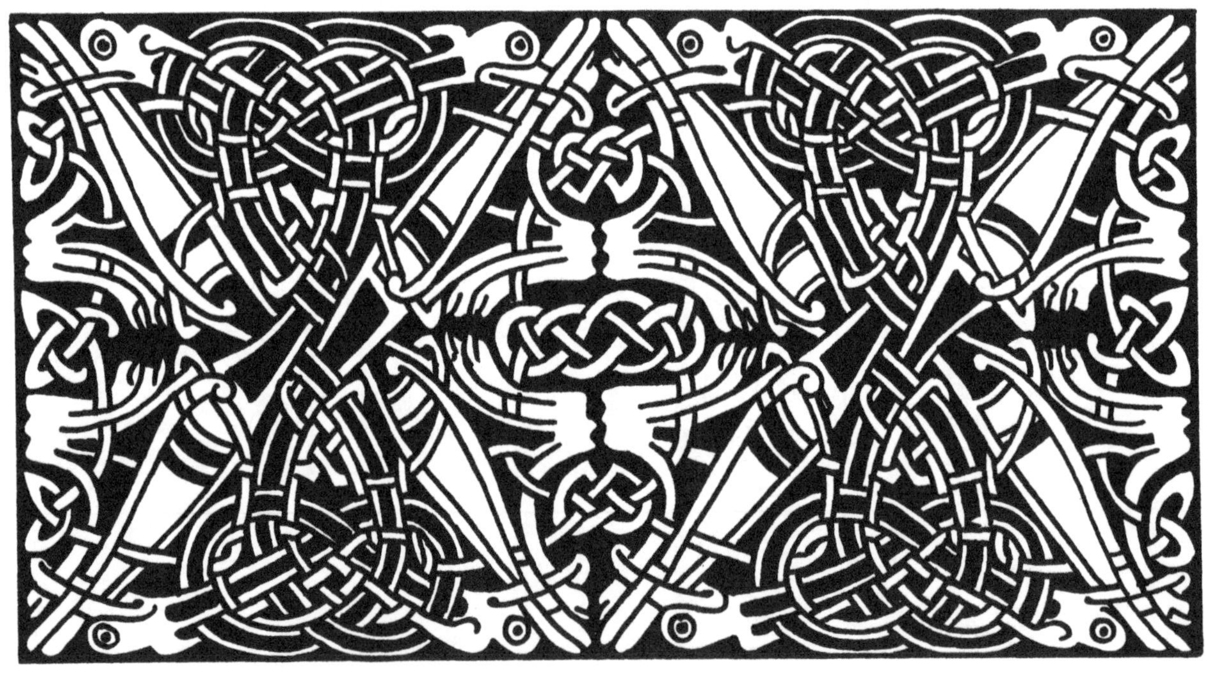

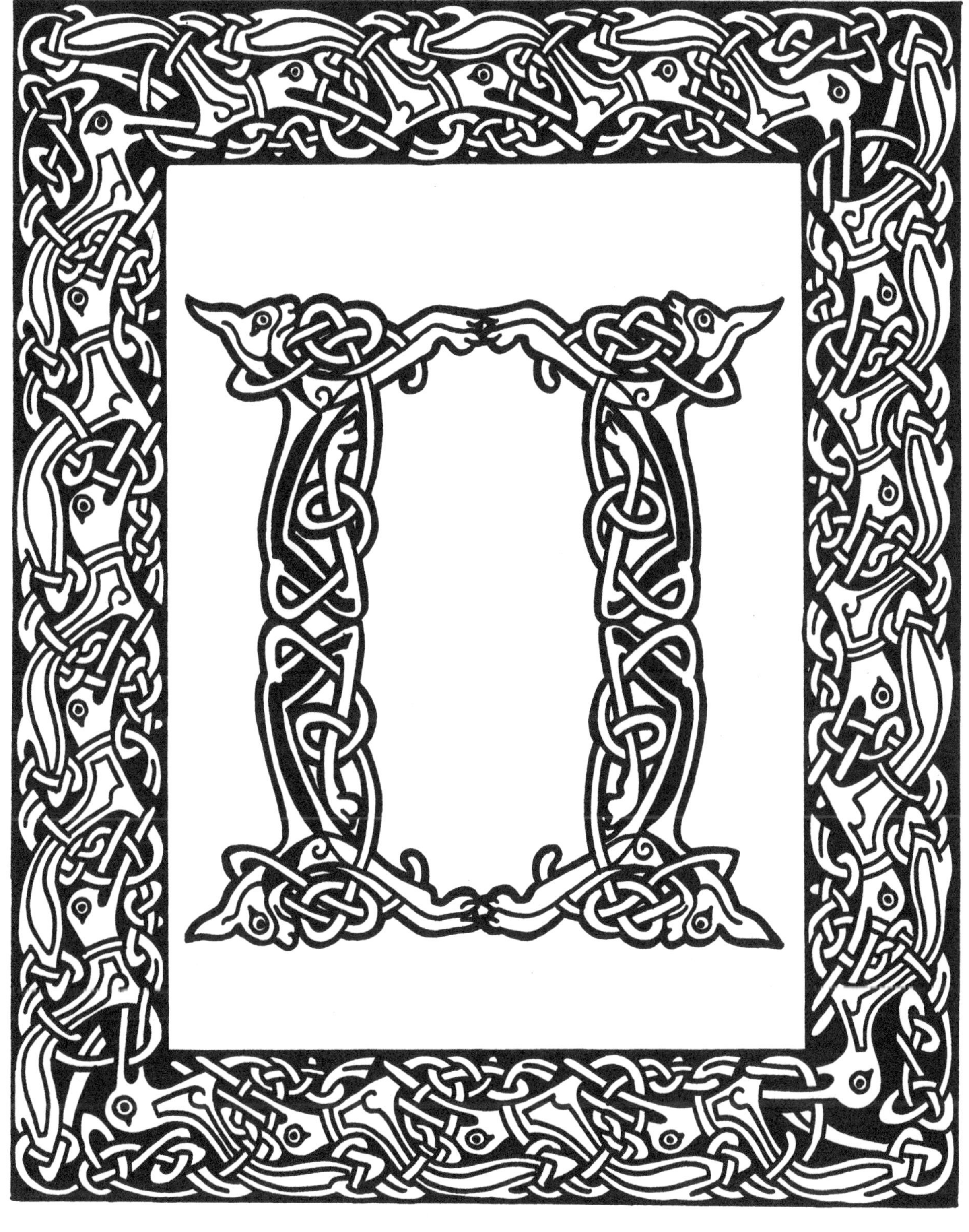

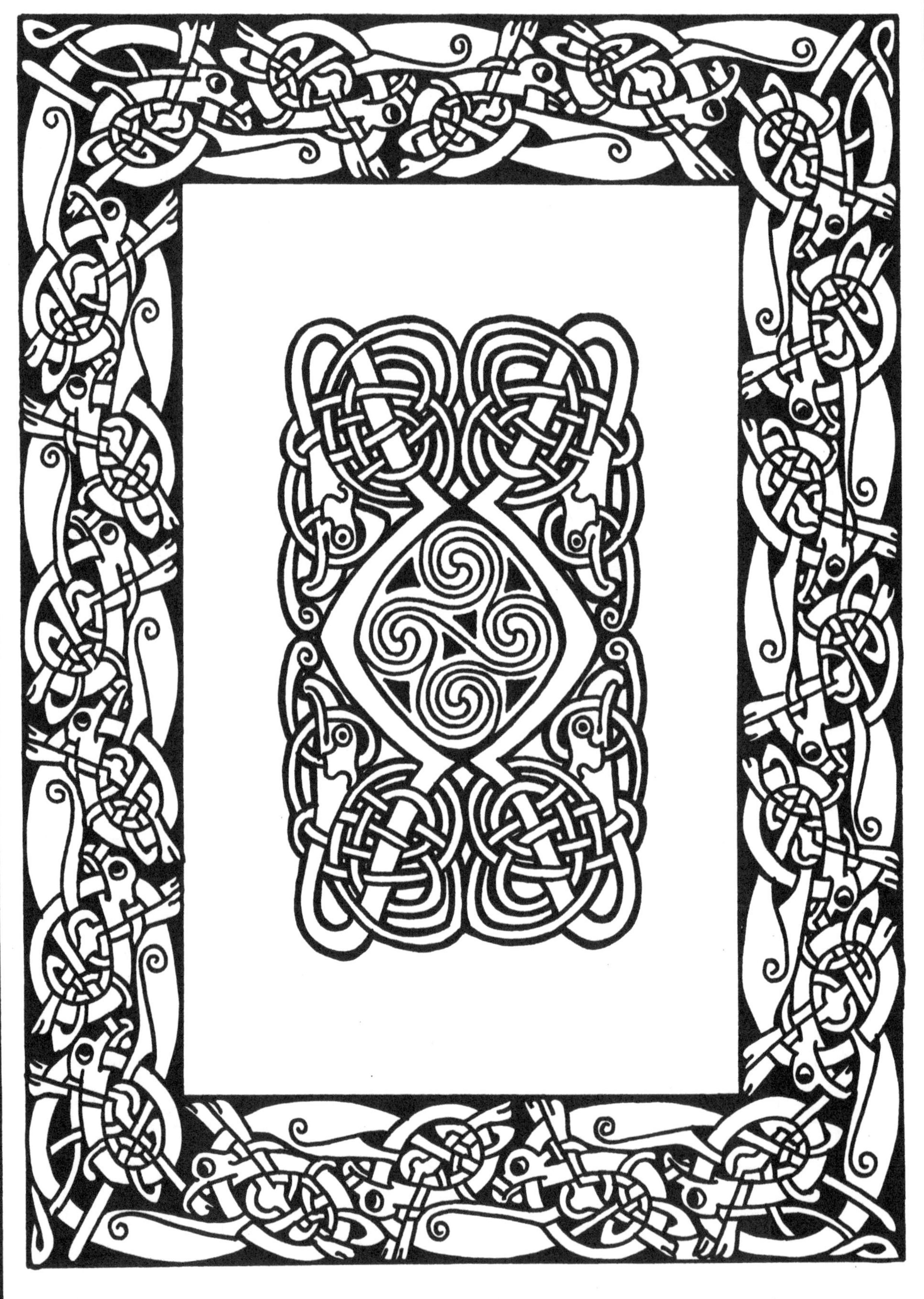